Hug yourself

Happy

Hug yourself

Happy

(Kids do - So can you)

A Life-changing
L'il Snuggle Book For Adults

Stephanie Lisa Tara

Hug Yourself Happy

Layout and design by Ted Ruybal

No toxic materials were used in the manufacturing of this book.

Preserve. Conserve. Inspire. Teach.™

Stephanie Lisa Tara
CHILDREN'S BOOKS

Stephanie Lisa Tara Children's Books
San Francisco, California

Preserve. Conserve. Inspire. Teach.

ISBN Paperback: 978-0-692-78083-1
ISBN E-book: 978-0-692-81438-3

Printed in the United States.
10 9 8 7 6 5 4 3 2 1

For more information about the author, or the book, please visit: www.stephanielisatara.com.

Table of Contents

Introduction

"I need a hug!"

Kids say this a million times.

Ah, the simple brilliance of asking for what they need!

But everyone knows that kids are far smarter than adults.

Let's learn from them!

I'll go first:

"I need a hug!"

Now, your turn.

Go ahead, it's okay to ask for comfort. It's our natural right to be happy!

Let's remember our past hugs . . .

The GOOD ones . . .

. . . The BIG ones . . .

. . . The L O N G ones.

The first super-duper ***snuggle*** (a really long hug session)

(I'll bet you are smiling!)

Hugs are *yummy*.

Hugs are *delicious*.

Hugs are *happiness*.

So, why then, are we not hugging more?

As *people?*

As a *society?*

As a *world?*

And, more importantly . . . ***can we change this?***

(This book was written in answer to that question.)

Want to change your life forever?

Start hugging.

Impossible? Yes, lots of folks scoff at such a silly, simplistic act.

They recall quickie hugs; a second or two.

And, no results.

Well, they're right. After a second or two, there are no results.

They don't recall a warm, loving, full-body experience of pure love energy.

Because: *their hugs were too short.*

I understand—I had the same experience.

And then . . . *I tried a twenty-second hug.*

It was strange to take the time to do it, to be honest.

But I did it.

I took the time.

Guess what?

It's different.

It's . . . strange . . . because it changes you.

You literally—feel calmer. Then, happier.

You are astonished, frankly, at this tiny little action . . . and how it results in a warm, happy, love feeling inside.

It's almost . . . embarrassing, because . . . it is **SO SIMPLE.**

Like the peel-off stamp, you say to yourself, God Almighty! Why haven't I been hugging more all these years? Decades? My entire life?

Incredible, and true.

Sure, there will be naysayers, here. Folks who will laugh, roll their eyes.

Why?

I think people tend to over-complicate things.

I know that I do.

Just take a look at New Year's Resolution lists!

#1 to #10—A nice big list of thousands of hours of new commitments, new goals, new deadlines.

All to make us "happier" in the given year.

The list alone portends depression! "In ten thousand hours, I will be thinner, fitter, smarter, younger, better traveled, neater, more stylish and have a new house, new garden, new partner, new job and I'll learn Mandarin!"

Oh my goodness.

Okay: you can keep your lists folks, but may I humbly suggest taking twenty seconds away from your list—and simply try a hug?

Imagine it for now: ***A self hug.***

And, imagine, later—another twenty seconds, and hug your partner.

Then your **kids.**

Your **pets.**

Your **family.**

Your **neighbor.**

Humor me—if only for the first twenty-second hug.

You can still go back to your list, I promise you.

Now, hold onto that thought-picture in your mind!

HUGGING.

It's *simple, easy, quick.*

I like simple—*you too?*

Love.

Give it a try.

It ain't hard, folks.

Costs nothing.

Try it? What have you got to lose?

Like a challenge? Okay here's one:

Try hugging for one month using the calendar at the end of this book.

Be honest, heartfelt.

My vow: if one month of hugging does not transform your life—I want to hear from you. Truly.

What happens when you hug for a month?

Your heart swells.

Think I'm kidding? You can feel it.

Your chest feels like it's expanding. You just feel filled up with love.

You understand your past.

Your see that your future is boundless.

***Dammit*—you just feel great all the time.**

So . . .

The BIG QUESTION:

Why don't we hug?
Why haven't we hugged?
What's wrong with us?

(Okay—I'll go first.)

Maybe I was afraid.

Okay, I was afraid.

For some reason I was afraid of how happy I would be.

Why?

Perhaps I felt I was too busy to worry about being happy?

You too?

It is quite normal in our hyperactive, *go-go-go* society to keep . . . going, doing, achieving, persevering.

And to forget ourselves along the way.

I am here to tell you: You deserve a hug.

Right now—**give yourself a hug.**

Great!

You feel better, I know. A lot of people feel better.

And better and better and better and better. With each passing day-of-hugs.

I interviewed hundreds of people for this book.

I could only choose a few.

Folks—I cried an ocean of tears reading all of your expressions.

I too, was afraid to hug, afraid to be hugged, afraid of what hugging might do for my life.

Then——I ***STOPPED!***

Yep.

I stopped, then started anew.

Know what?

I woke up happy.

You can too! Got 20 seconds—***right now?***

We're gonna do this properly—***professionally:***

Put down this book (please smile at it first) but do put it down, near you.

Now, take your arms and wrap them around yourself.

Squeeze.

Squeeze tighter.

Squeeze as tight as you can.

GOOD!

Hold this pose *(yoga class flashback)*

Try to inch your fingers farther across your back as you spread your arms wider for a really big, deep hug.

Now, please count:

(1 Mississippi, 2 Mississippi, 3 Mississippi . . . silently count to 20 Mississippi)

Okay, let go.

Feel it?

You feel the calm, the peace, the joy, the relief, the **HAPPY** inside you?

How ridiculously easy was that?

How can a hug do that? Can I get some hug analysis here?

Yes you can:

OXYTOCIN.

Sound it out, then put your sounds together . . . the word flows off the tongue like happy syrup. I write children's picture books in verse and I am a huge fan of fun-to-say words like this. Dr. Seuss was, as well.

OXYTOCIN.

Oxseetowsin.

It just feels ***yummy*** in your mouth.

So, what is it?

Oxytocin is the hormone released when you hug for 20 seconds or more.

A hormone? Yes. Also, a neurotransmitter.

Scientists call it a hormone/neurotransmitter that once released creates a feeling of happiness in the body.

So, back to how we can all hug ourselves happy . . .

HUG LAB:

Spend 20 seconds reading the news headlines.

Then spend 20 seconds hugging someone.

See? ***Wow, huh!***

Our point of view as hugger, has changed.

The point of view of our huggee has changed.

Stress reduced.

Heart rate calmed.

Things got a little better.

We hugged ourselves happy.

You may find, once you start hugging, that your hug-o-meter starts to expand.

More! More! More!

You may become a hug glutton.

"Let's all turn to our neighbor and give a nice long hug, I will count to 20 . . ." I said. Magic. They settled right down."

Author Testimonial:

One of the best parts of writing books for small children is reading those books to large groups of them. One of the hardest things about reading books to large groups of children is getting their undivided attention. One year, at an exceptionally large New York City event, I tried something new . . . the kids looked exceptionally squirmy. ***"Let's all turn to our neighbor and give a nice long hug, I will count to 20 . . ." I said.*** *Magic. They settled right down. They were smiling and happy. They were ready to listen. And, they were ready to hear. After the show, mothers complimented my hug methodology worked with the large crowd of children.*

I had a methodology?

I had a methodology!

I put on my lab coat:

Research suggested a **hug-arithm** (*hug algorithm*) of ***twelve 20-second hugs*** a day as the way to truly impact my happiness.

240 seconds of my day. Yep, I had time for that.

I created a journal of hugs, and I broke them down into categories:

1. **Self hugs :20**
2. **Husband hugs :20**
3. **Kid hugs :20**
4. **Dog hugs :20**
5. **Friend hugs :20**
6. **Stranger hugs :20**
7. **Tree hugs :20**

Some of you may be laughing at tree hugs, but ya know? Try it first. Laugh later.

Lab results?

I felt incredibly happy. Elated. Lighter. Sweeter.

I had hugged myself happy.

You can too.

I have a 31 day planner for you to scribble in, at the end of this l'il hug book.

Give it a chance, folks.

Blame it on me if you want!

"This San Francisco mom has me hugging trees and strangers . . . go figure . . ."

We all want to be happy.

It is our natural right as human beings.

We tend to compartmentalize happiness.

Yep, we do.

We assign **HAPPY** to Thursday at 7:23pm, after we have finished our To-do lists of 42,000 things.

Right?

It's strange, *isn't it.*

We go on vacation to simply be-inside-happy.

We say to ourselves, for the next ten days I will be inside happy.

Then we return to our responsibilities.

Right?

WRONG!

Folks—you deserve to be happy all the time.

You deserve a hug—all day long!

And guess what?

People around you deserve hugs from you.

That's the coolest part of about hugging.

It works both ways. In two directions. To give is to receive.

Beautiful, huh?

Hugging doesn't get you anything specifically: hugging prepares you to do anything you dream.

So many popular books today tell us how to many things to prepare for happier lives:

De-cluttering our living spaces!

Walking/pedaling to our jobs!

Eating only vegetables!

Eating only fruits!

Eating only grains!

Living in nature!

Living off the grid!

All of the above are amazing life changes for sure but none of them strikes at the core of being essentially happy: **LOVE.**

With love, we can do all of the above.

We can achieve our New Year's Resolution lists.

We can embrace our partners, families, neighbors, even strangers not because we have a de-cluttered life, but because we have allowed ourselves to feel love.

How about this: ***first hug the heck out of your life partner.***

Then set about to de-clutter your home together.

I promise you, the de-cluttering will be sweeter, and have deeper effects after the hug.

Take yoga.

I'm a life long practitioner.

Love it.

It centers me, calms me, helps me to see the bigger life view.

And when I add a big scrumptious twenty-second hug to my practice on my mat?

With a teacher or co-yogi?

My practice enters a new level of meaning.

I am smiling.

I am happy.

I am loved.

You see?

Insert any activity, sport, hobby into the above scenario.

Same end result.

Life-before-hugging is very different from life-after-hugging.

This sound familiar, below? (Scenes from my life)

First I buy stuff.

Then I toss stuff.

Then I get a pet.

Then I get another pet.

Then I get a new hairstyle.

Then I cut off the new hairstyle.

Then I buy a new outfit, bicycle, cookware, bedding.

Then I de-clutter the new outfit, bicycle, cookware, bedding.

(Folks, all I really ever needed—was a twenty-second hug!)

That simple feeling of happy. **Joy. Well-being. Caring.**

Today, I still like "stuff", sure I do.

I just got a super cool new crepe pan! But I also hugged my husband super tight—before I made him a tasty crepe.

100% total difference.

I could have put green peas (he hates them) in his crepe and he'd have eaten them with love :)

This all sounds really terrific, Stephanie—but what do you personally bring to the topic of hugging that is different?

Well, I am the first children's author to spill the beans... to sing like a canary...I am the first to speak out publicly about hugging.

(Drumroll)

Listen up:

KIDS HAVE BEEN HUGGING THEMSELVES HAPPY AND EACH OTHER HAPPY FOREVER.

That's it.

Simple as *that.*

I see it at every book reading I do.

I see it at every library event I do.

I see it at every school event I do.

I see it at every bookstore event I do.

I watch it.

I observe it.

I marvel at it.

I am wow'ed by it.

And now I'm shouting it from the rooftops:

Kids hug themselves happy. *You can too.*

What's next?

We need to tell the world!

(Heck, the world may heal a little if hugging increases, so let's do our bit.)

Yep: get out there and spread the love.

Share the secret.

Start hugging.

Make it go viral.

1-2-3-*GO!*

Want to change your life, starting now?

Start hugging!

Peace out.

I interviewed a lot of amazing people for this l'il hug book and my heart has flip-flopped a million times over. I am so honored by all of your beautifully honest expressions.

Yes, it is possible to hug ourselves, each other, and the world—happy. Kids do it every day! I like to think of my children's books as little paper hugs a child can embrace. Shucks, I still read Dr. Seuss and giggle up a storm.

I recently arrived at age fifty, and one thought has plagued me; why aren't adults happier? Middle age had me less concerned with fading beauty and more concerned with fading faith about what truly makes us happy. But, several hundred hugs later—my faith was renewed.

My hug book is different from others in that as a children's disciple, I have learned from their wisdom, and, oh my, are those little folks smart! We were children once, maybe a little reminding is in order?

Perhaps that's where I can help you, xo

Hugs,

Stephanie Lisa Tara
Children's Author, Activist, Mom, Hugger

Congratulations!

You took the first step toward hugging yourself happy!

Now, how did your first self hug feel? Quick—first words that pop into your mind!

Use this space to jot down all the things you felt . . .

(Personal share: My first self hug words included some doozies; sunshine, giggly, lavender, baby powder, yummy, tenderness, apple pie, grandma)

☺ ______________________________

☺ ______________________________

☺ ______________________________

☺ ______________________________

☺ ______________________________

☺ ______________________________

☺ ______________________________

☺ ______________________________

☺ ______________________________

☺ ______________________________

☺ ______________________________

☺ ______________________________

Chapter 1:

Self Hugs

How do we hug ourselves happy?

There are many ways.

I like to begin at the beginning.

Now—if you would—***please go look in a mirror.***

Smile.

Good!

Thank you.

I now return to the wisdom of those persons

three-feet-and-under.

Author Testimonial:

Another book event starring me, this time Dallas. Hottest day of the year and I had an hour to fill. Telltale signs of tantrum was written on every kids face as they stood in line waiting to get their books signed. What to do? I remembered New York City. But, sweaty kids hugging each other? Then I saw her. A tiny girl in a bright yellow dress, with her arms wrapped tightly around her body.

She was hugging herself.

BRILLIANT!

I stood up from my table with the microphone; "Everyone! I need you **ALL** to do something very, very, very, important for me right now! I would like you to hug yourselves as tight as you can . . . while you are in this dreadful, horrible, terrible, yucky line!

The kids immediately started self-hugging. Giggling too.

Once again—*magic.*

Oxytocin was flowing.

It was a deluge flood, to be honest. I could see it.

My children's author mind saw it too . . . in a *Cat In The Hat* moment I saw Oxytocin molecules floating and smiling above the kids...they were tiny happy faces in a rainbow of colors.

It was way, way beyond cute. And, way, way beyond wise.

"As each toddler approached me they only unlocked their arms to shake my hand, then re-wrapped their arms around themselves."

Later, at home, as I sipped a cup of tea, I thought about the transformed line of self-hugging tots.

I stood.

I wrapped my arms around myself. Reached way back. Grasped fingers farther. I took deep yoga breaths (these are deep inhale-through-the-nose-breaths, exhale-through-the-mouth-breaths.)

I counted to twenty.

I unwrapped myself.

Ah!

A wonderful healing-sense-of-happy.

Are you ready?

I think you are ready.

It's time for you to commit.

Twelve twenty-second self hugs a day.

Let's do this!

***I did*, and I was hooked.**

It's easy folks, *hold yourself and smile.* You deserve it. Truth? Being hugged by another is *scrumptious.* But a good ole self hug is so easy and available.

All. The. Time.

Be kind to yourself!

Be loving to yourself!

Be your own best friend!

Go ahead: Fall in love with yourself.

You will find that this alone, is incredibly powerful for attracting others to love you too.

XO

H

T

Hugger Testimonial:

"Okay. First off: I've been self hugging for years. Boy oh boy was I relieved when I read this book—cuz I have had some very embarrassing experiences where I gave myself a hug in public and got caught. I am now hoping that self hugging will go viral—so I can exonerate myself! Yep, I was first caught in an elevator, at the advertising agency where I worked . . . after a horrid meeting with clients impossible to please. I knew my work was brilliant, our clients were just not art-smart enough to see it. I didn't just spend four years at the best American art school twiddling my thumbs! So, yeah, after a grueling presentation, with a room full of faces that said (Huh?) I hugged my humiliated self from the 80th floor to the 5th floor. Problem was I had my eyes closed. When I opened them, the clients and my boss—stood

staring at me outside the elevators. But—I truth is, I did feel better. So I didn't stop. Next I was caught in a restaurant bathroom after a particularly horrible first date—but the gal at the sink was kind enough to pretend not to see me. Then there was the car hug. Being flipped off by a cranky driver shouldn't have upset me, but it did. I just hugged myself in between gear shifts. On a flight to Berlin during the worst turbulence I had ever experienced—you know it, hours of self hugs and cocktails. I was at a Lakers game and it was moments to the buzzer . . . I instinctively self hugged as I watched the ball fly toward the basket. That time I was caught by an entire row of sports fans. I didn't care. ***I had already decided to come out of the hugging closet. Woohoo for a book that celebrates this!"***

~Cindy Jones, Los Angeles, CA

"I had already decided to come out of the hugging closet. Woohoo for a book that celebrates this!"

H T

Hugger Testimonial:

"Someone once called me a Power Mom. It was meant as a compliment. 'What exactly is that?' I asked her. 'You do it all! All the time! Perfectly!' she answered. Wow, I thought to myself. I do it all, perfectly, all the time. That's a mighty job description. True enough, as moms, we're pre-wired to be loving, and to give endlessly. We love everyone around us. All the time. Nobody knows about the secret Mom Batteries we charge ourselves on every morning—which accounts for our go-go-go appearance! Actually, though? Just once, I'd love it if someone would cut my food up for me. Run a bath for me. Brush my hair and tie it up with ribbon. You know, while the Mom Battery Charger is charging. Okay—one day, I opened an email from my local yoga studio. The title was: Immersion in Love—for Mothers. Maybe? I thought. I bought a mat. And . . . then, magic. There in a class of twenty, were others in the power mom workforce. From washing dishes to managing

companies to washing laundry to logging more driving hours than New York taxis to morphing into passion queens for our husbands in the evening. Yes! I was home. Ninety minutes of bliss, all about finding inner nurture within a life of nonstop giving. But then an amazing thing happened in class. During a pose, where my arms were wrapped around my torso, I found I could not let go. I did not transition to the next pose with the rest of the class. I stayed, ***locked in a self hugging pose.*** *The teacher looked at me but did nothing. I sat down on my mat and stayed in my newly invented self hug yoga pose. Without knowing it—I had actually taken the next step. I had crossed the self love rubicom. From that day to this, I end all my yoga practices with a nice big comforting self hug.* ***What I love about self hugs, is that they are private little hugs that are different because these special hugs say that we think we are special. Try it! You'll be surprised."***

~Cathy Ann Stanton, Fairfax CA

"What I love about self hugs, is that they are private little hugs that are different because these special hugs say that we think we are special."

H

T

Hugger Testimonial:

"I'm a guy. We don't self hug. Ever. I manage an accounting firm, I watch football. I work out in the gym on weekends. I'm also a family guy and I adore my wife and kids. And, my dog. I hug my family constantly. Why would I hug myself? I mean, after a dozen beers maybe? Nah. Even then. So last summer a strange thing happened. I was driving home from a business trip, and my cellular battery had died. I stopped at a restaurant and had dinner, and plugged my cell into its charger. Suddenly, the phone started bleeping. Like crazy. I looked and saw, in horror, dozens of calls, texts, from my wife and kids. My parents. My best friends. Terror grabbed at my heart. I'd never known such fear in my life. I grabbed my phone and hit voicemail, to listen. The phone was frozen. Not

moving. I tried to shut it off, nothing. Frozen, with 36 calls and texts frozen along with it. I was in a horror film. Before jumping into my car and driving 100 mph home, **I did a crazy thing. I hugged myself. It just happened. I did it, tightly. I said aloud, 'Bill, calm, it will be okay.'** *I drove 60 miles in a half hour when the phone un-froze itself and I retrieved the messages. My dog had been hit by a car, and was in the hospital. Folks, I hugged myself again, I just did it. The PS to my story? Harlo, my terrier, recovered. I recovered. And—I am a new man."*

~Bill Danesky, Allentown PA

"I did a crazy thing. I hugged myself. It just happened. I did it, tightly. I said aloud, 'Bill, calm, it will be okay."

Fun Exercise

Houston—*we have lift off!*

Welcome to your first full day of quality self-hugging: You will notice something amazing—your hugs change and evolve as they progress . . .

The first hug has its own energy. Then comes the second hug . . . a little different! Perhaps easier, more comfortable. Are you like me—by the end of the day, my eighth hug was a dandy! I couldn't wait.

Use this happy space to record all your feelings! Words, phrases, sentences—scribbles, illustrations, cartoons . . . *let your happy flow* . . . ☺

8am self hug:

☺

☺

☺

9am self hug:

☺

☺

☺

10am self hug:

☺

☺

☺

11am self hug:

☺

☺

☺

12pm self hug:

☺

☺

☺

1pm self hug:

☺

☺

☺

2pm self hug:

☺

☺

☺

3pm self hug:

☺

☺

☺

4pm hug:

☺

☺

☺

5pm hug:

☺

☺

☺

6pm hug:

☺

☺

☺

7pm hug:

☺

☺

☺

8pm self hug:

☺

☺

☺

Chapter 2:

Spouse/Significant Other Hugs

You're hugging yourself and you love it!

You've fallen in love with yourself!

Yay!

Now it's time for the next step...

If you would, go find your significant other.

Look at this person, smile.

Tell them that you would like to hug them, for twenty lovely seconds.

Step toward them, smile, embrace, snuggle in there, tighter.

Hold.

(1 Mississippi, 2 Mississippi, 3 Mississippi . . . 20 Mississippi)

Step away slowly, gently.

Smile.

Good!

Now, ask your significant other, your husband, your wife . . . how they felt. From the first moment to the end of the twenty seconds.

Tell them how you felt from the first moment to the last second.

It's all okay folks—this could be your first twenty-second ***hug-with-a-purpose*** so it may have different residual feelings that those other impromptu hugs-in-the-moment.

Here we are **CREATING** a specific moment. We are making time for hugs. A pointed, conscious decision. Our goal is to hug up some happy, hug up some oxytocin hormones.

Sure it's easy to hug when we win the lottery. But this book wants to teach you to hug at all the other times. To put hugging into your day.

Awake.

Brush teeth.

Make coffee.

Hug.

You see?

☺

Kids have *BFFs*.

We need to think of our significant other as a BFF.

Our best friend forever. Inside this sacred, safe space—we can give and receive these amazing Oxytocin-rich hugs. The happiness we so need.

Simple, sweet, honest.

Passion is great, folks—the more the better: but let us first start with a simple hug that gives without expecting anything in return. Just a *wrap-around-squeeze* that says I love you. Feel this delicious squeeze, and feel your oxytocin levels rise.

The simple act of hugging goes a super long way to keeping your relationship happy and healthy.

It is easy to forget—so don't. Hugging is the non-verbal intimacy that makes relationships thrive.

It is connection, feeling close to your special person.

Just like with self hugs, hugging your significant other results in oxytocin hormones exploding in both your hearts.

That can lead to all the places you might wish it to . . . yes, *oolala!* But healthy relationship always begins with loving kindness, from there it blossoms into whatever you can imagine.

☺

Go ahead: Fall in love with your significant other!

Author Testimonial:

I married my best friend. Everyone always said this was a terrific way to start a life together. For many years it was terrific. Our careers blossomed, we shared everything together because, well, we liked all the same things as most best friends often do. Then kids came. And things started to change. As they often do. The notion to hug was just natural for us, pre the Hug Revolution that came decades later. We had always hugged, and so we simply continued this practice. It helped, enormously. It is interesting to talk about it now, as we married so young . . . but when I look back and reflect on it all today, I have to admit that it wasn't the 'grande passion' that carried us through the years. It was the friendship, unshakable. The energy we had in our hugs. Romeo & Juliet aside, ***I now believe that, at least in our case, those unbreakable hug squeeze reminders saw us through difficult times. Oxytocin saved us.*** *What can I say? It's true.*

"I now believe that, at least in our case, those unbreakable hug squeeze reminders saw us through difficult times. Oxytocin saved us."

H

T

Hugger Testimonial:

"My husband and I had grown apart. It had been a slow process like so many people experience. No big fights, no affairs, just that deathly quiet thing that happens as couples become overwhelmed by obligations and forget each other. Our lives were schedules. Our private time was penciled in around family events, business events. From the outside we looked happy. And then came that anniversary dinner. Best place in town. I wore my favorite dress. My pearls. My red lipstick. Why did I burst into tears, then, over dessert? I didn't know, and neither did my husband. He looked so sad. Yet, he also looked like he understood. We paid the bill, went home. 'What is happening" I asked him. 'I am not sure,' he answered. But we knew. Somehow the light had gone out. He leaned over and hugged me then. At first I thought it was a goodbye hug, and this made me cry again. But the hug lasted. It changed into something else. It ended and I will be honest here, it was a very small thing. A very small thing, on a day

of big things. It was not an epiphany moment. It was a tiny subtle moment that I did not understand until the next day. In the morning, I hugged him again. Same thing, a gentle hug at first, then a tight squeeze as if we were school chums. We both laughed. Another small moment. No conclusions drawn, nothing changed or even fixed. It was odd—a lone hug from my spouse, no strings attached, no pledges made. Just that closeness. Hearts together, squeeze. We kept doing this for a few days. Things became easier. Lighter. I started to research hugs on the internet. I read about a gal in San Francisco who was doing hug research for a book. I contacted her and shared our story. I guess all I can really say to everyone reading this, is that you must try it. Don't just read about it. Don't scoff at it. Try it. Don't expect epiphany changes. Do expect subtle changes. ***Hug your partner, every day for a week, a month. Then tell me you don't feel differently. I promise you—you will."***

~Delilah Wilkins, Boston MA

"Hug your partner, every day for a week, a month. Then tell me you don't feel differently. I promise you—you will."

H

T

Hugger Testimonial:

"Being gay takes courage today. For parents, it can be challenging. When I came out to my mom whom I love more than anything in the world, my knees were shaking. Funny, she didn't flinch. Her face didn't change. Her smile deepened. The cross she wore around her neck sparkled as brightly asit had before, as if she—and God—approved. ***She hugged me then. I'll never forget the hug. It was silent. But it said a thousand things.*** *I went home and hugged my partner Jack. I told him about mom. He and I made a pact to hug every day, and to remember mom's wisdom. It has been ten years, and we still return to our hugs daily. Amen."*

~Ben Levinson, San Francisco CA

"She hugged me then. I'll never forget the hug. It was silent. But it said a thousand things."

Fun Exercise

Ask your significant other how they felt after the hug.

Do this as a screenplay dialogue . . . finish the sentences . . .

Hug research matters!

Hugger:

The hug made me feel ______________________________

____

__________. (finish sentence)

Hugger:

The hug made me feel ______________________________

____

__________. (finish sentence)

Chapter 3:

Kid Hugs

You're on a hugging roll . . . nothing can stop you now!

You've fallen in love with yourself!

You've fallen in love with your significant other!

Now, let's fall in love with your children!

Hug ideas for kids:

☺ **Good morning! (:20 hug)**

☺ **Good night! (:20 hug)**

☺ **What an awesome job you did! (:20 hug)**

☺ **Thank you! (:20 hug)**

☺ **Could you help me with this? (:20 hug)**

☺ **I'm sorry you are sad . . . (:20 hug)**

☺ **Please share with your friend . . . (:20hug)**

☺ **Please don't throw your toys . . . (:20 hug)**

☺ **You have a beautiful smile! (:20 hug)**

☺ **You are talented! (:20 hug)**

☺ **You are creative! (:20 hug)**

☺ **You listen very well! (:20 hug)**

Hug results for kids:

- ☺ They feel better about themselves and their environment
- ☺ They become loving themselves
- ☺ They enjoy practicing forgiveness
- ☺ They become smarter, IQ rises
- ☺ They experience a brand new sense of security, safety, trust
- ☺ They are generally happy
- ☺ They experience pain relief
- ☺ They have lowered feelings of negativity
- ☺ They feel less lonely
- ☺ They are far less frustrated
- ☺ They are less anxious
- ☺ They are open to sharing feelings
- ☺ They are less fearful
- ☺ They are energized with a surge of energy

Hug results for babies:

(Babies are pre-language creatures so non-verbal hugs that say love are paramount)

☺ **Babies are calm and relaxed and at ease**

☺ **Babies have better circulation, muscle development**

☺ **Babies enhance their immune systems**

☺ **Babies sleep better**

☺ **Babies have lower stress, anxiety**

☺ **Babies experience higher tolerance for baby-issues like colic, teething**

☺ **Babies digest better, breathe better, and fill their diapers with more ease**

There are not enough pages in this book to express how important hugs are to a child. Along with your child's one-a-day vitamin should be a nice healthy dose of oxytocin . . .

A, B, C, D, Calcium, Iron, Oxytocin!

"After the story ended, my child said it was so much easier to feel the sadness with a hug around her."

Author Testimonial:

The Velveteen Rabbit is a lovely story to read but it does pull at heart strings and tears often accompany the beautiful lesson that teaches us. I tried a bear-hug-whilst-reading when doing the research for this book. I gathered my little girl into my arms and we read together, aloud. Sure enough . . . as the rabbit's hair was loved off . . . I heard a sniffle. I hugged my little girl tight—but did not say a word . . . who am I to interrupt the brilliant Margery Williams? ***After the story ended, my child said it was so much easier to feel the sadness with a hug around her.*** *And then she was happy. Wow!*

Hugs kids love:

- ☺ **Bear Hug:** One hugger is taller than the other. The short hugger stands straight against the tall hugger who may stand straight or slightly curved over the short hugger. The tall hugger wraps his/her arms around the other's shoulders while the other hugs around the waist or chest for twenty seconds.

- ☺ **Cheek Hug:** Can be experienced while sitting or standing. Each hugger turns towards the other and press the sides of their face together. For the hug to be most effective each hugger should ensure that they are relaxed by breathing slowly and deeply. One hand can be used to support the other's back while the other hand supports the back of their head. This hug stirs feelings of happiness and kindness. Twenty seconds.

- ☺ **Sandwich Hug:** Appropriate for both parents and a child. The two adults face each other with the child in the middle facing either parent. Each adult reaches towards the other's waist and hug. This hug gives the child a sense of security especially if he/she is experiencing negative emotions. Twenty seconds.

- ☺ **Heart-centered Hug:** This is the highest form of hugging. With this hug each person directly looks at the other eyes while facing each other; the parent can kneel to face the child. The arms are wrapped around the shoulders or back. Twenty seconds.

A hug repeats a message over and over and over to your child without saying a word:

"You are my love and my life and always will be."

Silent, effective.

XOXO

HT

Hugger Testimonial:

"It was the first day of preschool and I was nervous. My first job in a classroom of my own. I wanted it to be perfect. Years of study, years of planning, assisting, observing. Now was the moment. My classroom was brimming with friendly bright colors, each corner a special place of exploration. Calming ocean music played from the ceiling, where streamers of blue and green blew gently. My bunny chewed a carrot stick in her cage. Then they arrived—my students. They looked happy! I was thrilled. Each came in with their parents and I greeted them all with a smile and a hug. We settled on the welcome carpet and held hands in a circle. Just then the classroom door opened. A latecomer came in. My heart stopped when I saw the child's red eyes. I led the boy to the rug and we all said hello. Then he sat down and put his face in his hands and wailed. He kept on wailing louder and louder. At that very moment—our principal came into my classroom to greet my new class. How could this be happening

to me, I thought in horror. All my training went out of my head as I watched the child howl. The other kids started sniffling too. So—I stood and walked directly to the boy and gathered him up in my arms. I squeezed. Tighter and tighter. I looked around at the kids on the rug and asked them to choose a friend—and give a hug, just like I was doing. I told the kids to make it a tight one—or it won't count. The boy started to hug me back. He poked his head up and saw the other kids hugging. ***Then I stood up and asked the kids how it felt to hug. The little boy shot his hand up first, 'It made me happy when I was sad,' he said.*** *Later, the principal spoke to me and asked where I learned this emergency hugging method. I told her that the idea came to me that I could hug the crying away, at least temporarily. I didn't know what the boy's history was, nor did I really know anything about him. I just decided to try a spontaneous intervention-hug in a crisis situation. This is my particular hug story and I am glad to share it. Sometimes simple—is best!"*

~Jackie Moreland, New York NY

"Then I stood up and asked the kids how it felt to hug. The little boy shot his hand up first, 'It made me happy when I was sad,' he said."

H

T

Hugger Testimonial:

"Being a single dad is not easy. When my wife passed away, I felt like my world was ending. It was only the help of family and friends that carried me through the darkest moment of my life. My children were my reason to live. Yet, I was suddenly thrown into a life of managing every aspect of their little lives, a four year old, a seven year old and a twelve year old. The management of these three wonders was more challenging than running my law firm. Drop off at school, pick up from school, after school activities, PTA, field trips, weekend events, teacher meetings...even with the help of babysitters, I was soon overwhelmed. I read childcare books. I read child psychology books. I watched child rearing programs. I asked moms for advice. But what saved me in the end, was hugging. Because the truth is—I couldn't do it all. But I could offer the love of a dad who tried. That's what

hugs tell kids. When I failed at something, I just grabbed my kids and hugged them. No words at all. I hugged my kids and they hugged me. I insisted on hugs every morning and after school. And at night before bed. And before all of our activities. It became a habit that I found I needed, as a 47 year old suddenly single dad. It just helped. ***Yeah, I had heard about the free hugs for strangers thing somewhere in the headlines, but like most people—I didn't think much about it. Until I needed a hug myself. And I needed a hug more than anyone I know.*** *Hugs gave me sanity, they helped me process through pain. I wanted to share my hug experience with my kids and I hope that any other parents out there that may be suffering as I did, perhaps can gleam some comfort from my story.*

~Ben McKnight, Tampa FL

"Yeah, I had heard about the free hugs for strangers thing somewhere in the headlines, but like most people—I didn't think much about it. Until I needed a hug myself. And I needed a hug more than anyone I know."

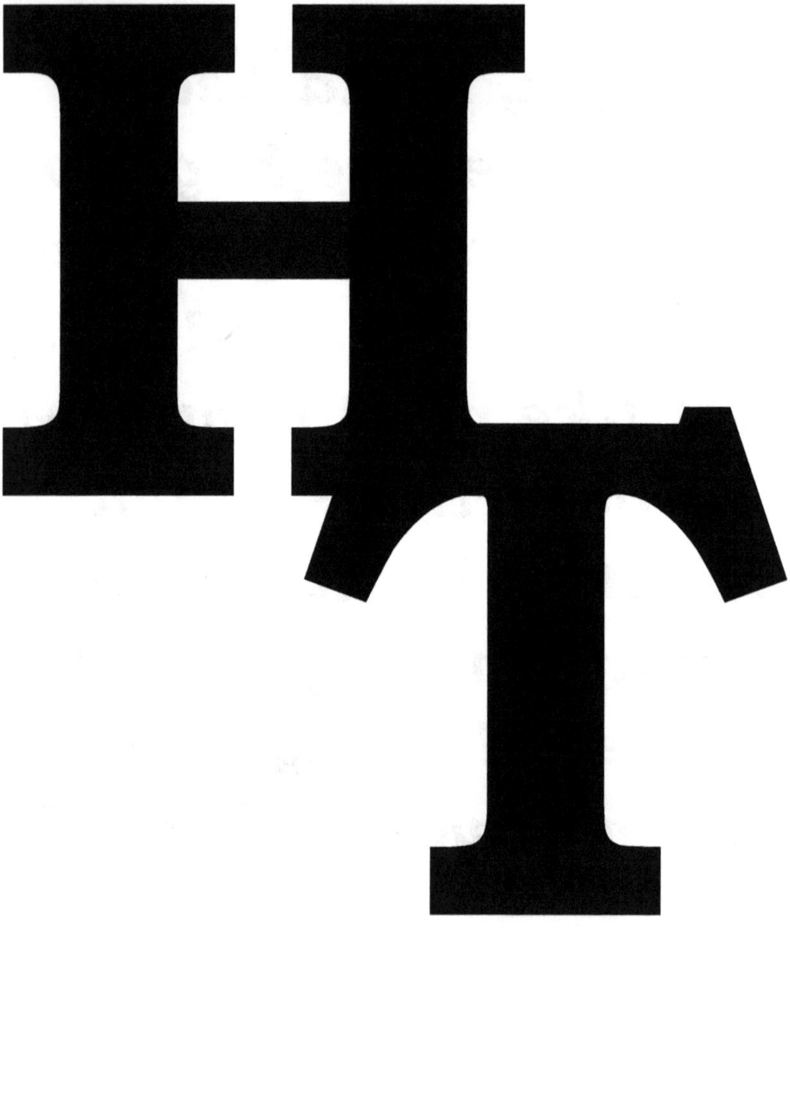

Hugger Testimonial:

"The refugee crisis has been talked about in the media at length. Many opinions. Here is mine. Our church asked for help for families that had arrived from Syria asking asylum. As a parish member, I felt I had to look into this. I attended the church meeting, gave money and went home. I said to my wife, after I put our sons to bed, that I thought maybe, there was more I could do. My wife called and arranged for a dinner. The Syrian woman and her sons met us a local restaurant and we dined, amidst broken conversation. Her tired eyes were those of someone decades older than she was. I asked she and her sons to stay the night with our family. The next day, I took her boys to a baseball field with my own sons. The boys couldn't speak

to each other—but did speak to each other if you understand my meaning. Boys, cheers, homeruns, smiles. We hugged after the game and have kept our weekend ritual. In my small way, I impact people in need, I give them some happiness. Sometimes it is the smallest act that has the biggest force. ***I can only tell you that these kids are huggin' up some amazing baseball love every weekend and it's totally amazing.***"

~Joe McDonald, Kansas City KS

"I can only tell you that these kids are huggin' up some amazing baseball love every weekend and it's totally amazing."

Fun Exercise

Please write down your kid (s) names in the heart.

Underneath the heart, write a list of areas that you feel challenges your child. (Maybe it's sleep issues, doesn't like veggies, has trouble listening, sharing, switching activities)

Now: Devote an entire day to twelve wonderfully delicious, compassionate, caring, deep, delightful twenty-second hugs with your child. Hug the child both randomly and at the specific times when their challenges come up. Take mental notes.

Later: Beneath your list, write down how things changed for your child, after individual hugs . . . as well as after an entire day of hugs.

Wonderful!

1. ______________________________

2. ______________________________

3. ______________________________

4. ______________________________

5. ______________________________

Chapter 4:

Pet Hugs

You've hugged everyone on two legs around you!

You are smiling.

You are laughing.

You are in full joy.

But how about those—on four legs?

Woof!

Meow!

You know whom we are talking about: the ones who love you unconditionally and without hesitation.

It's time to howl about the awesome benefits of hugging our pets!

Our four-legged-family members are all love and affection . . . and speak 'touch' far better than 'talk.'If you doubt this try "telling a pet" you love them.

Then, try petting and hugging that same pet.

See? Talk is cheap. ☺

Time for science: Oxytocin levels between owners and pets **SOARS** during bonding time.

Huh? My cat has oxytocin?

Yep—all mammals do!

In fact, levels are so high that . . .

☺ **Hospitals sponsor comfort-animal programs where dogs are brought in to soothe sick patients.**

☺ **Doctors endorse comfort dog prescriptions for those suffering from depression, anxiety.**

☺ **Elderly homes contract with animal rescue centers to pair older folks with dogs awaiting adoptions.**

☺ **Children diagnosed with autistic disorders respond well to animal love therapies that use petting, hugging techniques to inspire natural bonding.**

Hug benefits for pets:

☺ **They experience oxytocin**

☺ **They have palpable stress reduction**

☺ **They are noticeably more content**

☺ **They are less sick**

☺ **They feel empowered, have self esteem at the dog park**

Now,

what would your pet say to you today, if he could talk?

Be honest.

I'm sure my Jack Russell Terrier, Toby, would say . . .

"Stephanie, I'm a little Jack Russell terrier mix with a too-large head and too-short legs who had been living at the San Francisco Animal Rescue Shelter for over a year. Then you—adopted me! I know you have a busy life, with many responsibilities, I see you tearing around the house as fast as any Jack Russell I've ever seen . . . but if you have some time to pet me and hug me, like you used to, I would very much appreciate it.

I love you."

~Toby

Recognize anything?

It's the same principle, again.

Self.

Significant other.

Kids.

Of course I knew my little ten-pound pal needed me. And of course my schedule could accommodate twenty quality seconds.

Effortless.

Quick.

Profoundly satisfying.

"The amazing thing is that it mutually benefitted both of us. That's the magic of hugging. It works two ways. Oxytocin is produced in human bodies and doggie bodies."

Author Testimonial:

Toby Day!

I made a list of Toby's favorite activities. I devoted one day a week to each one. A hike. Fetch in the park. Doggie playdates with the neighbor. An extra helping of FreshPet. Sleeping in the den by the heat vent. Before each activity I gave Toby quality hugs. I knew I had other things to do but I made a conscious effort to 'make it up to Toby', for all the times I knew that he had waited for me. ***The amazing thing is that it mutually benefitted both of us. That's the magic of hugging. It works two ways. Oxytocin is produced in human bodies and doggie bodies.*** *While I expected to feel pressed for time, I instead found I was just* **HAPPY**. *Truth!*

H

T

Hugger Testimonial:

"My name is Mary. I am 93 years old. I live at Happy Acres Nursing home, here on the beautiful coast of North Carolina. I have had a good life, my four kids are all grown and in their lives, they visit me with the grandkids, they call and send me letters and cards. The grandkids come for holidays. I love my family. But when I say my family, I must include my Nora. Nora has become for me, a life companion. Someone I cannot live without. She is kind and gracious. Nora listens with the patience of a best friend. She waits, if I need to dry a tear. She waits if I need to stop and rest awhile. ***When I open my eyes, there is Nora, waiting next to me, big brown eyes open. And always the darling cuddles, Nora adores cuddling.*** *Once, when I*

had a problem with my heart, Nora went to fetch the doctors. It was 2am. She went and got a team and saved my life. Nora is everything to me now. She walks with me beside my wheelchair. She sits in my lap, in the gardens outside and smells the flowers with me. I tell her about my life, long ago. About my dreams and sorrows. I have never known a kinder soul. Does it matter to me that Nora is an eight pound poodle? Not in the slightest. I do wonder how I did without dogs for most of my life. How silly of me. I am now making up for lost time."

~Mary Flanders, Charleston SC

"When I open my eyes, there is Nora, waiting next to me, big brown eyes open. And always the darling cuddles, Nora adores cuddling."

H

T

Hugger Testimonial:

"I'm a loner. I spend a lot of my time hiking and seeing nature. I have never owned a dog because I honestly don't think I could be a very good pet Papa. Well, one year ago, I was walking the Appalachian trail, and I came upon a ragged beast. I thought it was a wolf. But, it was an abandoned dog. Left there, just outside of Shenandoah National Park. He looked like he was near dead. Problem was, I only had enough food left for me. Nevertheless, I shared my food with him. Okay, prepare yourselves: this ragged beast who had, obviously, had a really hard life and likely been treated fairly poorly by humankind—proceeded to follow me. Along the trail. I didn't encourage him. I didn't discourage him. Then, one night, when temperatures

dropped to zero, I let him into my tent. **It was cold, and there he was, a fluffy portable blanket that I could hug all night. Well, that night connected us. He stayed with me, all along my journey.** *At several points I was not in a good place. After all, I was not as fit as I should have been for arduous hiking, and I was older. Yet, my new friend was unflinchingly faithful. I could have stood on my head and acted crazy, he would have barked and wagged his tail. This is love. My two cents, for a book about finding something more in this world.*

~Rick Nester, Shenandoah VA

"It was cold, and there he was, a fluffy portable blanket that I could hug all night. Well, that night connected us. He stayed with me, all along my journey."

Fun Exercise

Inside of the speech bubble, please pretend your pet can talk. Write what he would say to you today. Be honest, like I was.

Read what you wrote.

Then,

go find your pet and do some quality 1-on-1.

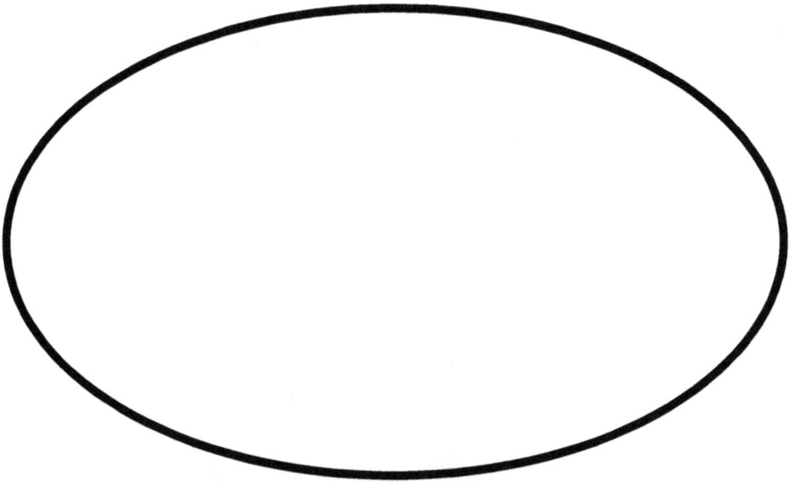

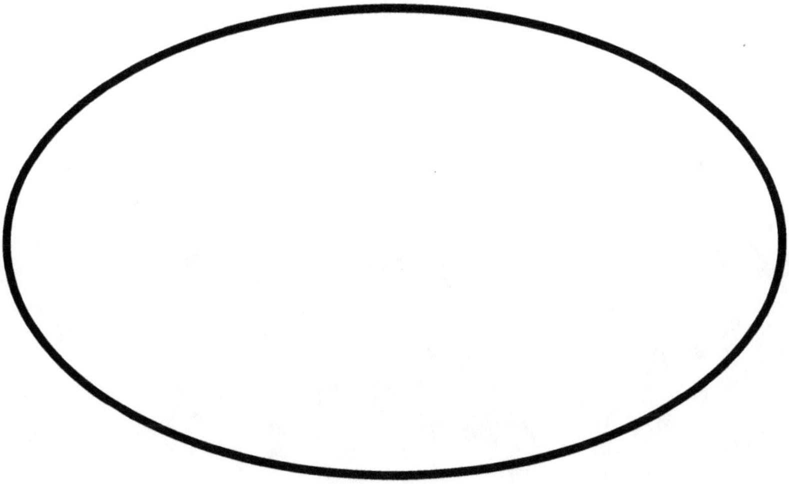

Chapter 5:

Friend Hugs

You're a Hug Monster now . . .
Your arms are permanently outstretched . . .

You love yourself!

You love your significant other!

You love your kids!

You love your pets!

The time has come folks,—go outside your home and spread the love, the gratitude . . .
time to hug your friends.

The first hug after a Mommy or Daddy hug?

A friend.

To a toddler, a friend is like a family member.

A hug from a friend is a warm bath after a long day. They have a different quality from our self-hugs, significant-other hugs, children-hugs.

They are extra special in that these hugs are not tied by bloodlines.

No, these hugs have a different energy.

These hugs are entirely chosen—for we choose our friends.

Question:

What kind of friend are we? What do our friendships truly say about ourselves?

Hug Lab:

Let's find out. We will then find out who we truly want to be in the world.

"Do I think that hug was equal to twenty years of electronic contact? You bet I do."

Author Testimonial:

I hadn't seen a darling friend for twenty years. As we were both writers, we found great comfort enjoying the 'then-new' social media revolution that had the world writing. We kept in touch with texting on new Smart phones, we enjoyed electronic mail, social media, it was a joy to feel the literary connection still alive and kicking. As the years went on, our friendship stayed strong. Photos, sound bytes, links . . . live chats with Skype. Who needed to actually be in real time human company, I thought. Well, how wrong I was. Our reunion was one of the most moving experiences of my life. A hug that lasted long minutes in the middle of San Francisco airport. The years came rushing back. Our faces, now creased a little, our hair, peppered with a little grey, didn't affect the way we felt in embrace. All five senses came together in the oxytocin-drenched event. Am I grateful for the technological revolution? You bet I am. ***Do I think that hug was equal to twenty years of electronic contact? You bet I do.***

HT

Hugger Testimonial:

"I'm a writer, living in New York City. I have advanced degrees in literature, writing, poetry. I am unmarried, mostly because I am obsessed with writing the great American novel. I know, I know . . . you've seen this a thousand times before. It is strange, though, to catch this bug, this illness called the writing bug. It is not pleasant. Up all night, sleep all day, walking around with electronic notebooks trying to envision a story that might change how a generation thinks. Too vast? Too noble? Maybe. But at 26, I feel as though I must try. Grad school still tingles in my brain. I am motivated! I belong to many writing clubs. I do stand up readings. I do poetry jams. I am involved on every level with interacting with other writers and my work. Yet . . . I haven't been able to accomplish what I want. The breakthrough has not happened. Why? I think this every day.

Then, one day, at a coffeehouse in Greenwich village, a friend handed me my latest manuscript. She looked at me and hugged me. A long sweet hug. Then she told me her opinions. The good, the bad, the ugly. What was different? I just cannot tell you. I felt such affection from her and my ears opened up and truly heard her criticism. It clicked. It clicked! I went home, rewrote. I asked several other friends, to please, read my revised manuscript. ***I asked if they would communicate their feelings—first with a hug, then with a chat. I made a joke that I was one of those oversensitive writers . . . the hugs helped me receive critiques.*** *All I can tell you is something inside me changed. I was hearing what was said. I was inspired to improve. All of this because of the affection, perhaps affirmation of my efforts. A marvel.*

~Sandy Whitecastle, New York NY

"I asked if they would communicate their feelings—first with a hug, then with a chat. I made a joke that I was one of those oversensitive writers . . . the hugs helped me receive critiques."

H

T

Hugger Testimonial:

"A dear friend of mine learned she had cancer. Tragically, a recurring cancer. The years of remission had fooled us into thinking she was healthy for good. She kept the news to herself for a long time. Her absence at various school events should have been a red flag. I assumed she was just busy with her husband, four kids and two dogs. Finally, she invited us, her closest friends, to a dinner at her home. She gave us the news. Prognosis, not good. As you can imagine, there were many tears. And, there were no words to be said. Unless you have been in a situation like this, it is impossible to describe. The silence, the wordlessness . . . is truly deafening. Then, my friend stood up and walked to each of us, and have us a long hug. Of course it felt like a hug goodbye. But the strange

thing was that...we weren't crying. ***The hug, in and of itself, strangely left us feeling uplifted. Uplifted in a situation that was everything but uplifting.*** *Yet we felt better. After hugging, we told stories about our kids. About our husbands. Funnyisms that came directly out of the uplifting hug energy. I have since realized that the power that manifested that day—was this hormone so talked about in the news, oxytocin. I like to think it God's way of helping our bodies react to life's trials. God made us, and he injected us with this magic. Call it oxytocin, call it love, or call it compassion. Or all three. Anyway, my friend is still struggling with her illness, and we do not know the outcome yet, but we meet regularly and hugs are always a part of it.*

~Joanna Yarlow, Austin TX

"The hug, in and of itself, strangely left us feeling uplifted. Uplifted in a situation that was everything but uplifting."

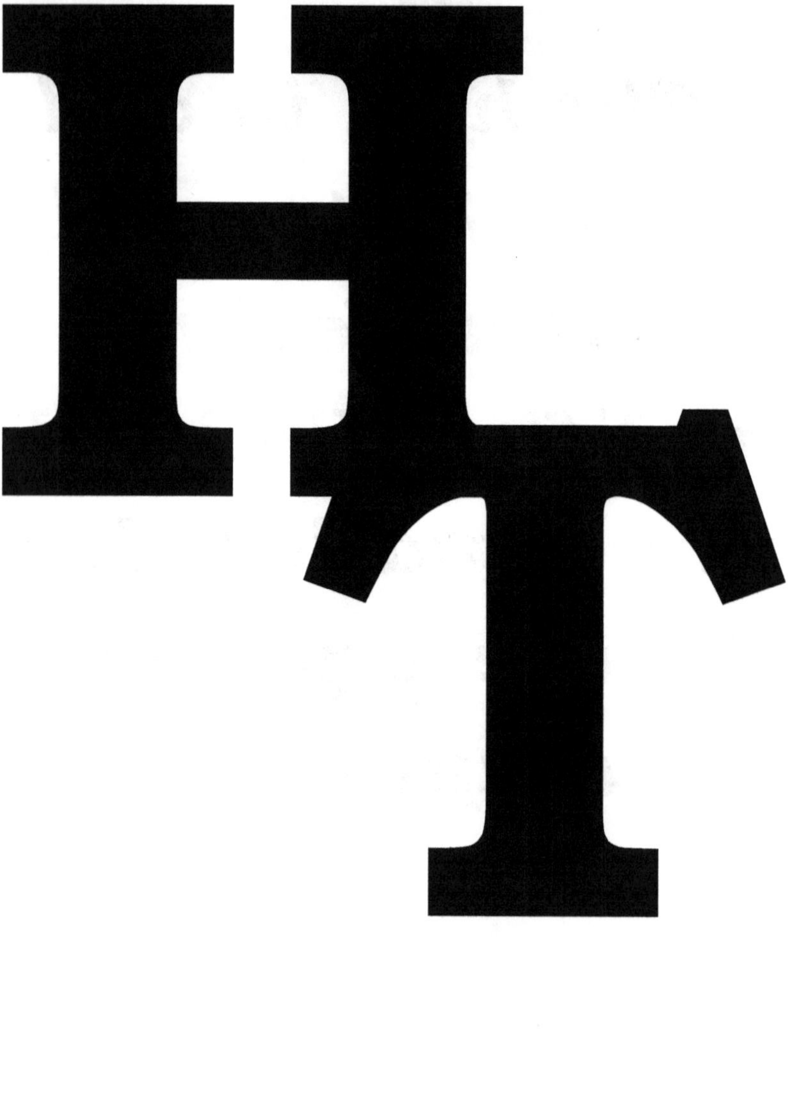
H
T

Hugger Testimonial:

"I turned 100 a week ago. I had made a bet with my grand children that I would live to see triple digits. I did it! This was a great accomplishment for me. The local newspaper wrote an article about my becoming a centurian. Yet, there is one sadness for me at having arrived at this grand age. My friends . . . have all passed on. I was explaining this to my daughter. She explained it to my grandson, Tim. Tim is very wise, the wisest four year old I know. Tim decided to have a friend party for his great grandpa. He invited all of his preschool pals to his house. When I arrived, they had formed a tiny line in front of a chair. I was escorted to the chair. Then,

one by one, the kids said hello to me and told me their names. They handed me a card they had made for me, and signed it . . . 'your friend, Suzy'. ***Then they hugged me. It had been so long since I had felt such sweetness. Who wants to hug an old man? These kids did."***

~John Stratton, Chicago, Illinois

"Then they hugged me. It had been so long since I had felt such sweetness. Who wants to hug an old man? These kids did."

Fun Exercise

Pick a good friend you would like to be closer to . . .

Next to each red heart, answer the questions. How much do you remember about your friend?

Hmmm. . .

Birthday?

Favorite book?

Favorite film?

Favorite food?

Favorite music?

Favorite sport?

Favorite hobby?

Greatest fear?

Greatest joy?

Chapter 6:

Stranger Hugs

You feel happy.

Everyone around you feels happy.

You have hugged yourself happy by hugging others happy!

CONGRATULATIONS!

Hey Love Bug—are you ready for a challenge now?

Your defining moment has arrived . . . and the world has never needed it more.

Question:

☺ ***How happy is the world you live in?***

☺ ***Perhaps, hugs can help.***

(**To all naysayers of hugging strangers: try it before you naysay*)

Let's look again at our *geniuses-under-three-feet.*

Hang out at a school, playground, camp, library, party. Pay attention to the little ones.

How amazing is their ease at *converting-a-stranger-to-a-friend?*

Children seem to inherently know that togetherness is better than separateness. They are willing to jump right in and start the process.

What is most fascinating—is the difference in children hugging themselves happy and adults hugging themselves happy: we seem to do it after-the-fact, after we have arrived at 'unhappy' a place that we of course placed ourselves.

Children have the wisdom to start the game with a hug, as they navigate their little lives and environments.

I was in a preschool once, when I saw a little girl hug another little girl. Then they played dolls.

I asked the child later on, *why the hug before the game?*

She said,

"I wanted her to play with me. So I hugged her."

Genius.

Perhaps world leaders might take a cue here; hug before aggression? Might be worth a try.

Back to the world of adults and the need for hugging.

Question: ***If a house in on fire—do you run and try to save your family?***

If the world is our family and everyone seems devoid of happiness, do we not try to save it?

Answer is entirely up to you.

I ask you to think here . . . as we arrive at chapter 7;

You feel happier.

You have affected your entire circle of souls with happiness.

Maybe . . . you can do more?

"She didn't understand me. She was old, and sick and afraid. I then gave her a hug."

Author Testimonial:

After a long flight from Germany, I landed in Canada, awaiting my connector flight to San Francisco. Delays. I saw a woman in a wheelchair, near the ticket counter. She was elderly. She rose from her wheelchair as everyone stared. She walked slowly to the counter. She started speaking in a language I was soon to learn was Farsi. She started to cry. Nobody knew what to do. I stood and went to the woman. I took her hands, and I said, 'it will be okay.' ***She didn't understand me. She was old, and sick and afraid. I then gave her a hug.*** *Then we went to sit down and she took out her cellular phone. She dialed. She spoke in Farsi. The she handed the phone to me. It was her son, in San Francisco. He spoke to me in English. He thanked me for helping his mother. He said he would be at the San Francisco airport when we arrived. Later . . . in San Francisco . . . his mother blessed me in a special way, she kissed my hands and said a prayer in her language over me. I will never, ever forget this as long as I live.*

When I got home, I thought about the happiness I'd felt. I'd recently turned fifty and life's big questions were filling my mind.

If only I was three years old—then I could tell the world how easy it was to hug!

I decided not to let this handicap stop me. And that's when it happened. I became a public hug ambassador.

Hugging a Stranger (*before*):

☺ **ASK FIRST:** Pose the hug request. Perhaps; *"I see you are sad, would you like a hug?"* Or, *"I'm reading a hug book and it suggests hugging strangers as a way to spread joy in the world. Might you be willing to allow me to give you a hug?"*

☺ **WHERE TO HUG:** Hugs are needed everywhere. Meeting spots are terrific. Coffeehouse. Bus stop. Park. Mall. Shopping center. Public safe spaces.

Hugging a stranger (*during*):

☺ Slowly lean forward, place your hands gently on the person's shoulders, place your heart next to person's heart. No other part of your body should be touching the person.

☺ Remain as you are without any further effort. No squeezing.

☺ Let your hearts synchronize, and just be in the moment. Count to twenty in your head silently. You will feel the connection. Oxytocin is flowing, being exchanged.

☺ Allow oxytocin to flood you with a sense of well being. It will be strange at first because the person is new and not your significant other, children or even dog.

Let it happen.

Remember your mission as a Hug Ambassador. Remember how you felt in chapter 1—your first self hug. Share that joy with your huggee. In purity. You may feel euphoric. A sense of peace. Belonging. Happiness. It will amaze you and your huggee. Smile. Enjoy.

☺ After twenty or so seconds, slowly lift your hands and step back from the person. Go back to your personal space, allow the person their personal space. Say "thank you" to your huggee.

Your hug is concluded.

H

T

Hugger testimonial:

"I sat in front of the news. Headline after headline telling me of all the hate in the world. Wars and disease and prejudice and sadness. I had just arrived in San Francisco from Dallas and was eager to start my new career in the art world here. Running a gallery of my own, my life's dream. And in such a magnificent city of love. Of open minded ideas, of compassion and acceptance. Yet as I watched the news, my heart sank. Why oh why were people so angry? So quick to hate. I flipped off the television. I went outside and looked. I really looked—at the passerbys on these steep streets of San Francisco. I started to smile at them as they trudged up and down. I found they smiled back. I walked about for two hours from the Haight to the marina, smiling at everyone in

the city. I got home and felt terrific. Ideas for my gallery were burgeoning in my head. The next day I saw a man on the corner of Ashbury, a block from my apartment. He had a FREE HUGS sign. He was asking for hugs! I had been smiling just the day before and here was a sweet soul hugging. I flew into his arms and hugged him for all I was worth. It was fantastic. I shared his sign, all that day and we hugged many, many people. He explained that free hugs and hug challenges had been popping up all over the world. I was so excited. We had a movement! We had a revolution. Amen. When I read this super cool book by this super cool San Francisco mom, I thought—kismet. It was meant to be. ***Let's hug ourselves happy! What a novel idea. Profound and meaningful and a propos. Bravo!"***

~Ivy Sticklby, San Francisco CA

"Let's hug ourselves happy! What a novel idea. Profound and meaningful and a propos. Bravo!"

H

T

Hugger Testimonial:

"I was standing on the subway platform in New York City, waiting for the train. It was a bitterly cold day, yet freakishly warm here deep underground in the tunnels. I had had a long hard week. My wife had lost her job, my job was uncertain at best. The 2008 financial crisis had many victims, not just us, I knew. Yet, I tried to keep faith. But you know how it is, one thing after another. Kids, cars, house... everything costs money. Still, I had hope. What does hope look like? I am not sure. If it is a color, then it is yellow, I think. As long as I can keep a shade of yellow in my being, I will be okay, I often think. That morning as I stood waiting for my subway to arrive, I saw a woman at the edge of the platform. The space where the cement

drops off and the falls a few feet down to the train tracks. The whistle blew in the tunnel. I am not sure why I looked at her at the moment I did. I am not sure why I saw no yellow in her at all. I am not sure of anything other than the fact that I ran. As fast as I could, I ran and grabbed her arm, snapping it back hard. It was only afterward, that I saw she wasn't wearing a winter coat, and that her clothes were dirty. I hugged her for all I was worth. I don't know why I did. But I did. **When she hugged me back, I knew I had done something important that day. A moment, a gesture.** *I don't know whatever happened to her. But I know that the power of that hug did something profound.*

~Henry Klein, New York NY

"When she hugged me back, I knew I had done something important that day. A moment, a gesture."

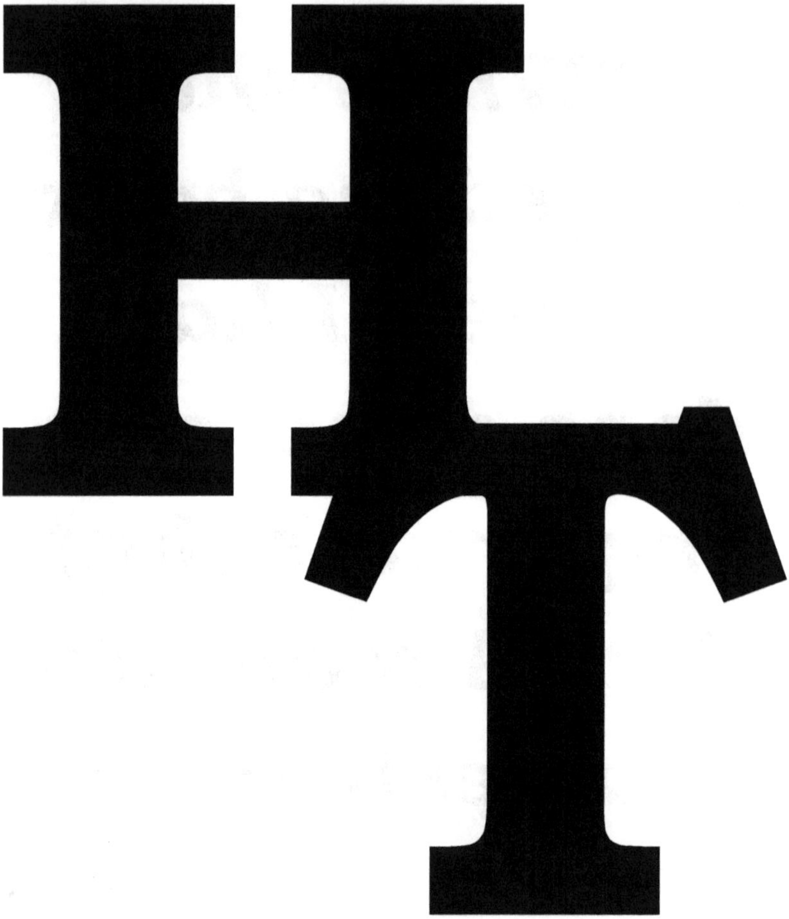

Hugger Testimonial:

"My story is a crazy one, but an important one to tell. You might have read it earlier, 2001, to be exact. My office in the World Trade Center was destroyed on September 11th. Along with the world, I went into a kind of prolonged shock. For days I wandered the city in a blur of pain at lost friends, at why I had been spared. A late trip to get a second coffee had saved my life. In the weeks and months following the attacks, I tried to piece my mind and my life back together. I was a New Yorker, born and bred, I wanted to embrace my city I loved in its time of need. It just happened, a few days later, when I

was standing in a cold coffee truck line on Bleecker street. Everyone was crying. I got my coffee, took a sip. I went to the woman in the back of the line and hugged her. Then, the next person, a man. And, the next, another woman. I cried too. For the grief was unfixable. ***But the hugs connected us, even in grief.*** *I cannot say I felt happy after hugging, I can say that I felt trust, connection and a link that was strong to these grieving people whose lives had been shattered.*

~Giovanna Sorrento, New York NY

"But the hugs connected us, even in grief."

H
T

Hugger Testimonial:

"My exams were over and I knew I hadn't done well. I was terrified for a lot of reasons, my family would be disappointed in me, I was disappointed in me. Harvard had proved to be too much for me. I am a quiet, shy person, and did not engage much in class. I levied all my strengths into assignments and exams. And now I felt my exams were a disaster. I was very despondent and spent a week in my dorm room. I finally emerged. I then spent a day in the quad, on a bench. One of my professors came by and saw me. She approached me and said she had read my exam and found it unusually enlightening. Philosophy, my favorite subject. My

essay on Locke argued against publically held opinion of his work. I hugged my professor hard and my gloom started to melt. Physical closeness is a thing I am not comfortable with, Chinese culture frowns upon it. But, here I felt so much better, all with embracing my professor. ***For the rest of the day, I searched out my professors and hugged them, asking directly for my exam results. This was so much better than hiding.*** *Some exams were as I thought, not great, but I was empowered to go and meet my destiny, and accept whatever fate had in store—after a hug. I felt I was able to do this after I felt the human touch that said to me that the professors acknowledged my efforts.*

~Li Na Wong, Harvard University, Boston MA

"For the rest of the day, I searched out my professors and hugged them, asking directly for my exam results. This was so much better than hiding."

H

T

Hugger Testimonial:

"My grandmother had died, and I was on a plane home. Three thousand miles were a long way to go, and the stewardesses kept coming over to ask if I needed anything. To be left alone—I wanted to yell, but didn't. The gentleman on my right noticed my sniffles, but was kind enough to stay buried in his book. Halfway across the country, I suddenly felt overwhelmed with never seeing my grandmother's face again. Or hearing her voice. I'd had a glass of wine, which I am sure helped the tears start to fall . . . but once they did, they didn't stop. The man in the seat next to me closed his book. He took off his glasses and turned to me. He touched my

hand. I held on tightly. Then he leaned over and put his arm around me, and hugged me to him. We stayed like that for a little while. I felt better. ***We never exchanged a word. The kindness of strangers—remarkable."***

~Rita Gomez, Bend OR

"We never exchanged a word. The kindness of strangers—remarkable."

Fun Exercise

Fill in the Hug Sign with whatever feels right to you.

Maybe it is simply, *"FREE HUGS"*.
Maybe it is, *"HUG CHALLENGE"*.

I had one Hug Ambassador write a short paragraph on her sign about her very first stranger-hug, and what it felt like.

I had another person write a prayer for the world; *FREE HUGS* written underneath.

Others use humor, *"I suffer from Hugitis—my doctor tells me I need 25 hugs a day or I will go mad"*.

A mom I know gave away *'Hug Pins"*—each pin said, *"Yay! I hugged a stranger happy today!"*

Go ahead, be creative.

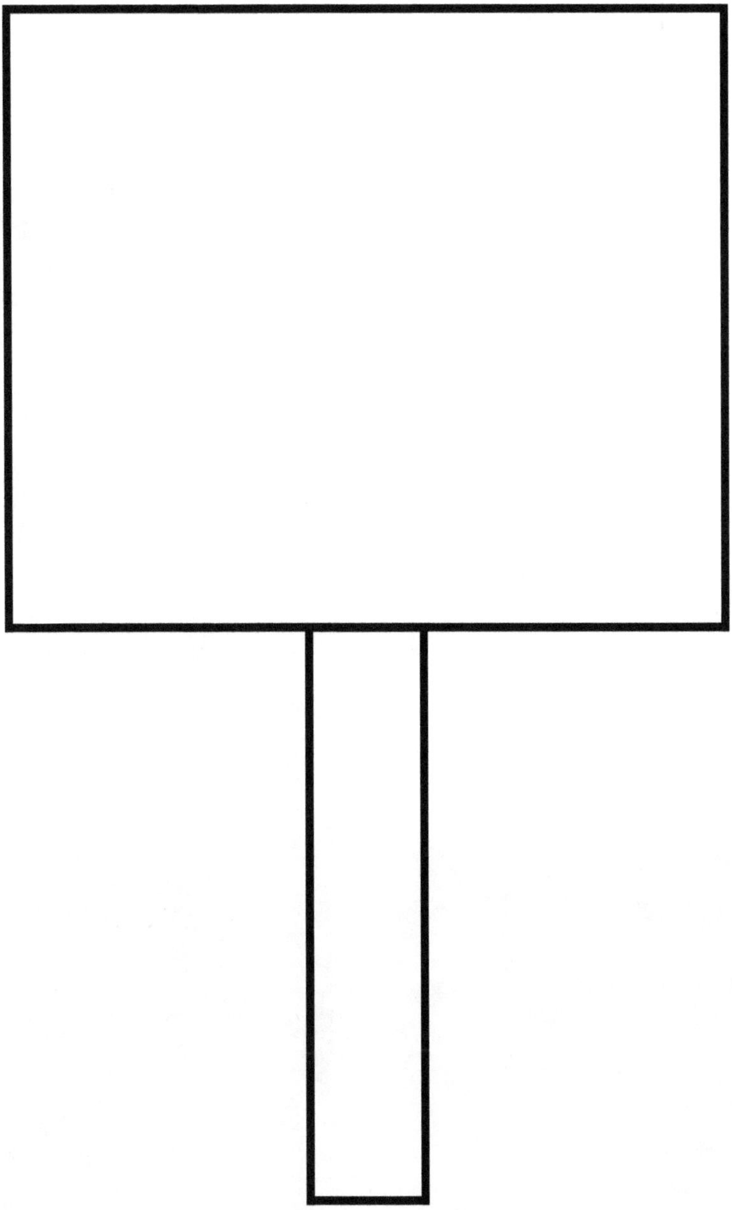

Chapter 7:

Nature Hugs

I am very proud of you!

You should be very proud of you!

The world is a better place because of you!

Look at all the love you have created in virtually no time at all:

☺ **Self hugs**

☺ **Family hugs**

☺ **Pet hugs**

☺ **Friend hugs**

☺ **Stranger hugs**

Whom have we forgotten?

Go to a window right now, please.

Look outside.

Mother Nature needs a hug, folks.

I will begin with the most huggable being in nature:

TREES.

Question: ***Have you ever, really, hugged a tree?***

I have.

IT IS MARVELOUS!

The case for trees and tree hugging is universal.

(Note to naysayers: try it first! Then decide.)

Consider:

Trees are organic, living things.

Ever seen the way your plants arch themselves toward the sun? Or, away from heat?

They are able to feel.

Science speaks:

The atoms that make up trees have their own unique vibrational patterns that are proven to cause positive changes in humans' biological behaviors when touched.

Tree vibrational theory has been tested with water: when drinking 10Hz-saturated water, our bodies' blood coagulation changes.

We, literally—

get good vibes from trees.

It's Mother Nature's oxytocin; in plant form. Cool, huh?

So when we hug a tree—*we are hugging ourselves happy with our own body's oxytocin, and we get positive vibes from the tree as well.*

And, I am sure the tree benefits too . . . I have been hugging my redwoods, just outside my home for years. They are always look happy.

Need more proof?

Let's look at history: Druids and Germanic pagans worshipped trees. Trees and forests are the fabric of many cultures. Folklore, and literature are filled with magical forest imagery . . . fauns, elves, pixies, trolls . . . have invited us into their tree worlds for thousands of years.

Why?

Well, trees just make people feel good.

And new studies show *tree hugging to fight disease* as our cells have amazing reactions from tree-contact in detecting and killing cancers.

Kids + nature = bliss

Schools in the San Francisco bay area have gardens. Gardening is a course considered as important as Math, Science and English.

Green spaces at schools are considered vital.

Chemical, spiritual interactions between kids and plants is well documented as a powerful antidote to psychological disorders and concentration levels.

Some schools have kids harvesting gardens and making salads for lunches. Others have kids planting seeds and naming the sprouts as they bloom.

Heck, folks—John Muir knew it.

"The clearest way into the Universe is through a forest wilderness."

We need nature . . .
as much as we need other people.

All of this together in a universal hug-ourselves-happy declaration.

We can only live outside of nature for so long.

We can only live outside of people for so long.

We can only live . . . without happiness for so long.

Disconnection is the root of pain, connection is the cure.

"But when I hugged her . . . a feeling of home came over me. I had come home. And Great Mother Redwood was there to greet me."

Author Testimonial:

After four picture books, I decided to try my hand at writing a middle grade novel for tweens. I knew I needed an amazing protagonist . . . one that would be inspiring, loving and unforgettable. Great Mother Redwood was a natural choice. Our family had enjoyed the magnificent redwood forest outside our home for many years. We lived just above San Francisco, home to Muir Woods, a grove of fantastic redwoods that enjoy the lovely San Francisco fog—a nourishing breath from the Pacific ocean that waters the trees and keeps them healthy. Eliza's Forever Trees was born and went on to sell millions of copies as kids everywhere fell in love with this matriarch of the forest, a tree that had lived a million years. But for me—the moment I most remember about writing that book, was the moment I actually—found her. Great Mother Redwood herself. My daughter and I took a new path in Muir Woods, this one led out toward the sea. It was steep. A little too steep, I remember, and this fact accounted for the sparse number of hikers. At the end of the path stood a tree that for all intents and purposes—was the greatest tree I'd ever seen. She wasn't bigger than those I'd encountered in Yosemite. Or wider than those I'd see far to the north. But she had a quality that is hard to describe. She just looked like a mother. She had a large space around her too. Maybe it was the way the sun shone on her, I am not sure. ***But when I hugged her . . . a feeling of home came over me. I had come home. And Great Mother Redwood was there to greet me.***

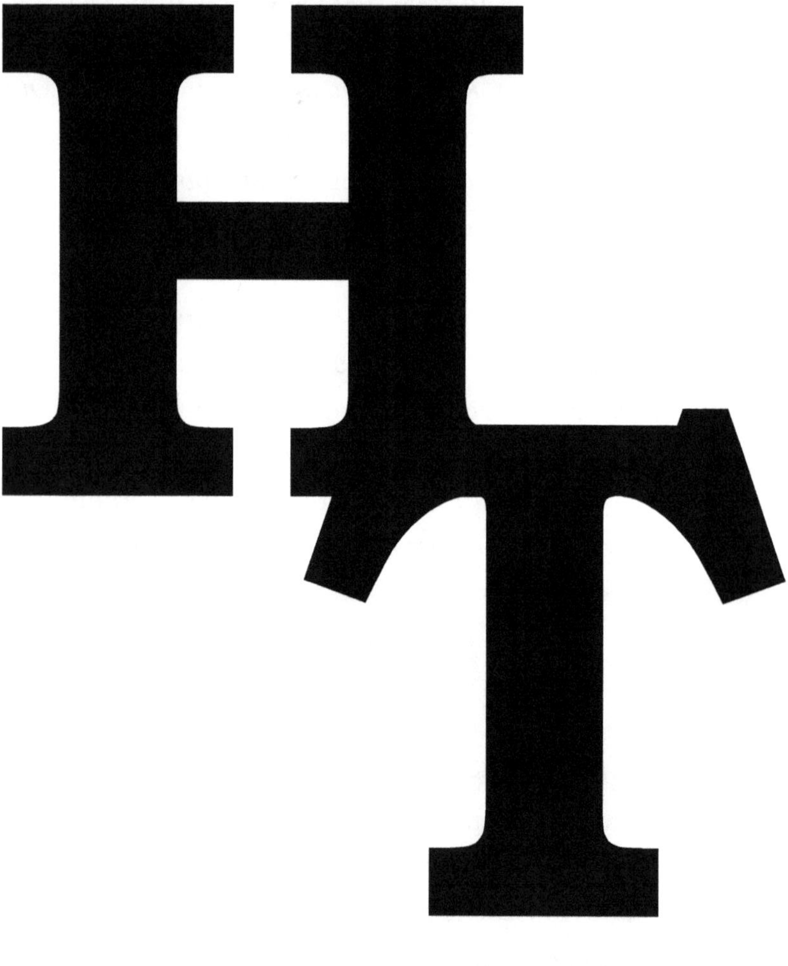
H
T

Hugger Testimonial:

"I have been called a freak. It is quite okay. I am rather flattered by the label. Being normal today is fairly freakish to me. I live Crescent City, which is the last town in northern California before you hit the Oregon border. I live in a redwood forest commune with other peaceful folks, near Jedediah Smith Redwoods State Park. We grow our own food, and share all we have. A lot of us are refugees of urban life who sought a better way. Some of us were struck down by disease and found nature to be our healing God. We live with the trees, we love them as family. I have been hugging trees all my life. Long before it became cool to hug them. When I heard

about Stephanie's book I asked around first. I find that this San Francisco mom has written many books for kids that preach love our planet. This new book about hugging ourselves happy, including trees and nature, just makes me smile. So many people walk the walk but don't talk the talk. This gal is living her words. ***We hug trees and have the joy of knowing God. I pray the whole world can embrace the earth and finally come home.*** *If you are sad, unhappy . . . man—take a walk in nature, brother. Breathe deep. Embrace a tree. Take your time. I promise good tidings."*

~Samuel Johnson III, Crescent City CA

"We hug trees and have the joy of knowing God. I pray the whole world can embrace the earth and finally come home."

H T

Hugger Testimonial:

"Forest Home School is my creation. My child was diagnosed with developmental delays. Countless hours with doctors all seemed to say, wait and see. Wait and see? I wanted to be proactive. I wanted to experiment. Not sit still and watch. So we did dance therapy, music therapy, art therapy, and sports therapy. But it was Laura herself who gave us the answer. She asked to see the trees. Which trees, I wondered, and Laura showed me her storybook. A forest story in rhyme, about a family of deer living in a forest. Laura's speech came slowly, and she didn't look at me as she spoke, she stared only at the trees, tracing their trunks with her finger. I told my husband about what had happened and we packed up that weekend for a camping trip White River National forest in Glenwood Springs, two hours from our Denver home. How to describe this? Laura was different in the forest. Her senses were sharp and she was

in focus with her surroundings. She listened, and responded to all she saw. She spent hours touching the bark of the trees. **She smelled the trees, talked to the trees and hugged the trees. The quiet majesty of these tall beings calmed her.** *As parents, we always look for any glimmer that says things might be okay. I am telling you, Laura was okay— that weekend. Her peacefulness astounded us. I am not saying she was cured. I am saying that the forest soothed her. My decision to home school Laura was an easy one. My decision to name our little home school was something I felt I wanted to do to help spread the awareness about how good nature is for our kids, all kids of course, but kids with learning disabilities especially. A new yet old—prescription for health. Yes, parents, we do have alternative choices for our kids who learn differently. The truth is in the pudding—it has truly helped our child."*

~Sandra Cunningham, Denver CO

"She smelled the trees, talked to the trees and hugged the trees. The quiet majesty of these tall beings calmed her."

Fun Exercise

Name the three trees.

Now, go outside . . . either in your yard, or local park, or local forest.

Choose three trees. Name each one. Find a distinguishing characteristic about each to remember them by.

And now—hug the tree, twenty seconds each. Same method as with people, embrace, squeeze, hold, release.

Make sure to do deep breathing as trees also purify the air around them expertly.

Keep a hug journal of your quality hug time with each of your tree friends.

Invite your family, friends and maybe even strangers to join you in your tree love.

Tree Name:

Tree Name:

Tree Name:

Chapter 8:

Conclusion

MY HISTORY OF HUGGING

I woke up the other morning, looked at my Hug Calendar and realized my one-year hugging anniversary had arrived.

I sifted through my twelve 31-day hug journals and just marveled. It was amazing to read them, to see how my commitment to hugging started, how it progressed, how it evolved . . . and deepened.

I am often asked if I was always a hugger. Strangely, I was inside—*but didn't know it.*

As a child, I was a very shy girl, a shy redhead I remember being called by others. The coined phrase comes from the Peanuts characters, the little redheaded girl who was too shy to speak.

When I really look inward and ask myself how and why I turned to hugging . . . I find I have to admit that I was always trying to fit in.

With my extremely bright red hair, I stood out physically—which is funny when I remember how I felt incredibly shy inside.

So, in my efforts to be accepted, even at the age of five, I remember being drawn to loving, confident people, people who showed affection and made me feel seen and heard and valuable.

I distinctly remember a little girl hugging me on the first day of kindergarten.

We had gone around the circle at circle time and I whispered my name—*Stephanie*—in the tiniest voice. Mary was next and she yelled it out proudly—***MARY!!!***—and I was so enchanted by her bravado, that I squeezed her hand.

She replied with an enormous hug that lasted several seconds.

Well . . . *I was happy all day.*

By first grade I remember volunteering to be a teacher's helper at recess. My job was to make sure everyone had someone to play with and that nobody was excluded.

By third grade, I was elected to be a big sister to the new kindergarteners, my job being to help them feel welcome.

I was used to greeting them daily with a hug.

In high school my mother signed me up to be a candystriper at a local hospital, which in those days meant teens in striped aprons that offered smiles, **hugs** and help to various patients.

By the time I reached adulthood, I was writing children's picturebooks for kids, in whimsical verse.

I am told that my baby sea turtle book goes to bed with many toddlers so they can "hug" baby turtle all night long.

So—though I did not plan it, or know it—I had been hugging since I was a child, and for all the reasons that make hugs so powerful.

Empowerment!
Belonging!
Acceptance!
Love.

LONGTERM MAGIC OF HUGGING

People have shared so many different stories with me about what happens for them, after hugs.

After just one hug, I am told that a window opens. A sunbeam sneaks inside. A smile tiptoes onto lips.

After hugging for a month—people say their perspective on all things changes.

And after hugging for a year—their way of life has transformed completely.

I know my life is changed: my first inclination is now to be compassionate, forgiving, loving.

Why?

The physical connection of hearts is a powerful oxytocin generator.

When one open heart sees another open heart—the two hearts beat together creating a magical energy. The oxytocin, or love gene if you prefer—is the spark.

What can I say friends, hugging changes how we behave.

It changes first responses.

Think about Facebook and why it became a culture the risks uber-connection. Friends. Outreach. Trust. Connection. Love. ***Virtual hugs!***

It could be called Heartbook—for it truly attaches two hearts together to create an energy that is very, very powerful.

Fascinatingly simple, isn't it?

Hugging gives us confidence!

Confidence spills from our beings.

Our walk changes, we smile all the time.

Hugging yourself happy means hugging yourself confident!

Try this: *think of a time when you received amazing news, something marvelous happened to you, and the feeling inside you was pure joy.*

Pure happiness.

You walked through your day beaming. When you came into contact with people—they couldn't help but absorb your happiness too, your happy-confidence was contagious.

It is the same with hugging: the confidence that hugging gives us, the feeling we have if being loved, seen, heard and valued—propels us to hug others—to give others that same gift we ourselves are enjoying.

It's a nuclear fission reaction

Hug → Love → Confidence → Share → Hug → Love → Confidence → Share

HUGGING IS A VERB

I love verbs.

I love action.

Words are terrific, and I make my life from them. But action does speak louder than words, and to make hugging really come alive in your life, you must actually do it, physically.

The good news is that it is **SO EASY.**

SO SIMPLE.

If you can make this verb one of your favorites, If it can become a part of your daily speech; walking, reading, sleeping, shopping, laughing, listening, speaking, praying, hugging . . . I think you will find your life will become happier, sweeter.

Hugging makes happy times happier. Hugging eases sad times with compassion. Hugging brings our loved ones closer. Hugging shares kindness with strangers. Hugging offers a way for our planet to heal.

Hugging promises to harness the power of love for all of us in our lives, manifesting happiness on a level never before seen.

Hugs,

Stephanie Lisa Tara

Sample:

31 Day Hug Journal

☺ Folks, your goal is *twelve* :20-daily-hugs at minimum

☺ Seven Huggee Groups;
Self | Kids | Partner | Friends | Pets | Strangers | Nature

☺ Pick three daily times | Jot down who got the hug by name | Jot down how you/recipient felt after the hug

Self

1. 6:30am, Stephanie, Cuddly____________________

2. 1pm, Stephanie, Anxious______________________

3. 11pm, Stephanie, Grateful, love________________

Kids

1. 7:15am, John, Content_________________________

2. 7:25am, Sue, Scared ___________________________

3. 3pm, John, sick, fever but loved hug ____________

Partner

1. 7am, Empathetic______________________________

2. 10:30pm, Stressed but in love__________________

3. ____

Friends

1. 2pm, Joe, Agitated but better after hug__________

2. ____

3. ____

Pets

1. 9am, Toby, Happy!______________________________

2. ____

3. ____

Strangers

1. 3pm, Older woman at market; thanked me for hug

2. ____

3. ____

Nature

1. 10am, redwood, feeling peace__________________

2. ____

3. ____

Day 1

31 Day Hug Journal

☺ Folks, your goal is *twelve* :20-daily-hugs at minimum

☺ Seven Huggee Groups;
Self | Kids | Partner | Friends | Pets | Strangers | Nature

☺ Pick three daily times | Jot down who got the hug by name | Jot down how you/recipient felt after the hug

Self

1. ____

2. ____

3. ____

Kids

1. ____

2. ____

3. ____

Partner

1. ____

2. ____

3. ____

Friends

1. ______________________

2. ______________________

3. ______________________

Pets

1. ______________________

2. ______________________

3. ______________________

Strangers

1. ______________________

2. ______________________

3. ______________________

Nature

1. ____

2. ____

3. ____

Day 2

31 Day Hug Journal

☺ Folks, your goal is *twelve* :20-daily-hugs at minimum

☺ Seven Huggee Groups;
Self | Kids | Partner | Friends | Pets | Strangers | Nature

☺ Pick three daily times | Jot down who got the hug by name | Jot down how you/recipient felt after the hug

Self

1. ______________________________

2. ______________________________

3. ______________________________

Kids

1. ______________________________

2. ______________________________

3. ______________________________

Partner

1. ______________________________

2. ______________________________

3. ______________________________

Friends

1. ____

2. ____

3. ____

Pets

1. ____

2. ____

3. ____

Strangers

1. ____

2. ____

3. ____

Nature

1. ______________________________

2. ______________________________

3. ______________________________

Day 3

31 Day Hug Journal

☺ Folks, your goal is *twelve* :20-daily-hugs at minimum

☺ Seven Huggee Groups;
Self | Kids | Partner | Friends | Pets | Strangers | Nature

☺ Pick three daily times | Jot down who got the hug by name | Jot down how you/recipient felt after the hug

Self

1. ______________________________

2. ______________________________

3. ______________________________

Kids

1. ______________________________

2. ______________________________

3. ______________________________

Partner

1. ______________________________

2. ______________________________

3. ______________________________

Friends

1. ______________________________

2. ______________________________

3. ______________________________

Pets

1. ______________________________

2. ______________________________

3. ______________________________

Strangers

1. ______________________________

2. ______________________________

3. ______________________________

Nature

1. ____

2. ____

3. ____

Day 4

31 Day Hug Journal

☺ Folks, your goal is *twelve* :20-daily-hugs at minimum

☺ Seven Huggee Groups;
Self | Kids | Partner | Friends | Pets | Strangers | Nature

☺ Pick three daily times | Jot down who got the hug by name | Jot down how you/recipient felt after the hug

Self

1. ______________________________

2. ______________________________

3. ______________________________

Kids

1. ______________________________

2. ______________________________

3. ______________________________

Partner

1. ______________________________

2. ______________________________

3. ______________________________

Friends

1. ______________________________

2. ______________________________

3. ______________________________

Pets

1. ______________________________

2. ______________________________

3. ______________________________

Strangers

1. ______________________________

2. ______________________________

3. ______________________________

Nature

1. ______________________________

2. ______________________________

3. ______________________________

Day 5

31 Day Hug Journal

☺ Folks, your goal is *twelve* :20-daily-hugs at minimum

☺ Seven Huggee Groups;
Self | Kids | Partner | Friends | Pets | Strangers | Nature

☺ Pick three daily times | Jot down who got the hug by name | Jot down how you/recipient felt after the hug

Self

1. ______________________________

2. ______________________________

3. ______________________________

Kids

1. ______________________________

2. ______________________________

3. ______________________________

Partner

1. ______________________________

2. ______________________________

3. ______________________________

Friends

1. ______________________________

2. ______________________________

3. ______________________________

Pets

1. ______________________________

2. ______________________________

3. ______________________________

Strangers

1. ______________________________

2. ______________________________

3. ______________________________

Nature

1. ____

2. ____

3. ____

Day 6

31 Day Hug Journal

☺ Folks, your goal is *twelve* :20-daily-hugs at minimum

☺ Seven Huggee Groups;
Self | Kids | Partner | Friends | Pets | Strangers | Nature

☺ Pick three daily times | Jot down who got the hug by name | Jot down how you/recipient felt after the hug

Self

1. ______________________________

2. ______________________________

3. ______________________________

Kids

1. ______________________________

2. ______________________________

3. ______________________________

Partner

1. ______________________________

2. ______________________________

3. ______________________________

Friends

1. ______________________________________

2. ______________________________________

3. ______________________________________

Pets

1. ______________________________________

2. ______________________________________

3. ______________________________________

Strangers

1. ______________________________________

2. ______________________________________

3. ______________________________________

Nature

1. ______________________________

2. ______________________________

3. ______________________________

Day 7

31 Day Hug Journal

☺ Folks, your goal is *twelve* :20-daily-hugs at minimum

☺ Seven Huggee Groups;
Self | Kids | Partner | Friends | Pets | Strangers | Nature

☺ Pick three daily times | Jot down who got the hug by name | Jot down how you/recipient felt after the hug

Self

1. ______________________________

2. ______________________________

3. ______________________________

Kids

1. ______________________________

2. ______________________________

3. ______________________________

Partner

1. ______________________________

2. ______________________________

3. ______________________________

Friends

1. ______________________________

2. ______________________________

3. ______________________________

Pets

1. ______________________________

2. ______________________________

3. ______________________________

Strangers

1. ______________________________

2. ______________________________

3. ______________________________

Nature

1. ______________________________

2. ______________________________

3. ______________________________

Day 8

31 Day Hug Journal

☺ Folks, your goal is *twelve* :20-daily-hugs at minimum

☺ Seven Huggee Groups;
Self | Kids | Partner | Friends | Pets | Strangers | Nature

☺ Pick three daily times | Jot down who got the hug by name | Jot down how you/recipient felt after the hug

Self

1. ______________________________

2. ______________________________

3. ______________________________

Kids

1. ______________________________

2. ______________________________

3. ______________________________

Partner

1. ______________________________

2. ______________________________

3. ______________________________

Friends

1. ______________________________

2. ______________________________

3. ______________________________

Pets

1. ______________________________

2. ______________________________

3. ______________________________

Strangers

1. ______________________________

2. ______________________________

3. ______________________________

Nature

1. ______________________________

2. ______________________________

3. ______________________________

Day 9

31 Day Hug Journal

☺ Folks, your goal is *twelve* :20-daily-hugs at minimum

☺ Seven Huggee Groups;
Self | Kids | Partner | Friends | Pets | Strangers | Nature

☺ Pick three daily times | Jot down who got the hug by name | Jot down how you/recipient felt after the hug

Self

1. ______________________________

2. ______________________________

3. ______________________________

Kids

1. ______________________________

2. ______________________________

3. ______________________________

Partner

1. ______________________________

2. ______________________________

3. ______________________________

Friends

1. ______________________________

2. ______________________________

3. ______________________________

Pets

1. ______________________________

2. ______________________________

3. ______________________________

Strangers

1. ______________________________

2. ______________________________

3. ______________________________

Nature

1. ____

2. ____

3. ____

Day 10

31 Day Hug Journal

☺ Folks, your goal is *twelve* :20-daily-hugs at minimum

☺ Seven Huggee Groups;
Self | Kids | Partner | Friends | Pets | Strangers | Nature

☺ Pick three daily times | Jot down who got the hug by name | Jot down how you/recipient felt after the hug

Self

1. ______________________________

2. ______________________________

3. ______________________________

Kids

1. ______________________________

2. ______________________________

3. ______________________________

Partner

1. ______________________________

2. ______________________________

3. ______________________________

Friends

1. ____________________
2. ____________________
3. ____________________

Pets

1. ____________________
2. ____________________
3. ____________________

Strangers

1. ____________________
2. ____________________
3. ____________________

Nature

1. ______________________________

2. ______________________________

3. ______________________________

Day 11

31 Day Hug Journal

☺ Folks, your goal is *twelve* :20-daily-hugs at minimum

☺ Seven Huggee Groups;
Self | Kids | Partner | Friends | Pets | Strangers | Nature

☺ Pick three daily times | Jot down who got the hug by name | Jot down how you/recipient felt after the hug

Self

1. ______________________________

2. ______________________________

3. ______________________________

Kids

1. ______________________________

2. ______________________________

3. ______________________________

Partner

1. ______________________________

2. ______________________________

3. ______________________________

Friends

1. ______________________________

2. ______________________________

3. ______________________________

Pets

1. ______________________________

2. ______________________________

3. ______________________________

Strangers

1. ______________________________

2. ______________________________

3. ______________________________

Nature

1. ______________________________

2. ______________________________

3. ______________________________

Day 12

31 Day Hug Journal

☺ Folks, your goal is *twelve* :20-daily-hugs at minimum

☺ Seven Huggee Groups;
Self | Kids | Partner | Friends | Pets | Strangers | Nature

☺ Pick three daily times | Jot down who got the hug by name | Jot down how you/recipient felt after the hug

Self

1. ______________________________

2. ______________________________

3. ______________________________

Kids

1. ______________________________

2. ______________________________

3. ______________________________

Partner

1. ______________________________

2. ______________________________

3. ______________________________

Friends

1. ______________________________

2. ______________________________

3. ______________________________

Pets

1. ______________________________

2. ______________________________

3. ______________________________

Strangers

1. ______________________________

2. ______________________________

3. ______________________________

Nature

1. ______________________________

2. ______________________________

3. ______________________________

Day 13

31 Day Hug Journal

☺ Folks, your goal is *twelve* :20-daily-hugs at minimum

☺ Seven Huggee Groups;
Self | Kids | Partner | Friends | Pets | Strangers | Nature

☺ Pick three daily times | Jot down who got the hug by name | Jot down how you/recipient felt after the hug

Self

1. ______________________________

2. ______________________________

3. ______________________________

Kids

1. ______________________________

2. ______________________________

3. ______________________________

Partner

1. ______________________________

2. ______________________________

3. ______________________________

Friends

1. ______________________________

2. ______________________________

3. ______________________________

Pets

1. ______________________________

2. ______________________________

3. ______________________________

Strangers

1. ______________________________

2. ______________________________

3. ______________________________

Nature

1. ____________________

2. ____________________

3. ____________________

Day 14

31 Day Hug Journal

☺ Folks, your goal is *twelve* :20-daily-hugs at minimum

☺ Seven Huggee Groups;
Self | Kids | Partner | Friends | Pets | Strangers | Nature

☺ Pick three daily times | Jot down who got the hug by name | Jot down how you/recipient felt after the hug

Self

1. ______________________________

2. ______________________________

3. ______________________________

Kids

1. ______________________________

2. ______________________________

3. ______________________________

Partner

1. ______________________________

2. ______________________________

3. ______________________________

Friends

1. ______________________________

2. ______________________________

3. ______________________________

Pets

1. ______________________________

2. ______________________________

3. ______________________________

Strangers

1. ______________________________

2. ______________________________

3. ______________________________

Nature

1. ______________________________

2. ______________________________

3. ______________________________

Day 15

31 Day Hug Journal

☺ Folks, your goal is *twelve* :20-daily-hugs at minimum

☺ Seven Huggee Groups;
Self | Kids | Partner | Friends | Pets | Strangers | Nature

☺ Pick three daily times | Jot down who got the hug by name | Jot down how you/recipient felt after the hug

Self

1. ______________________________

2. ______________________________

3. ______________________________

Kids

1. ______________________________

2. ______________________________

3. ______________________________

Partner

1. ______________________________

2. ______________________________

3. ______________________________

Friends

1. ______________________________

2. ______________________________

3. ______________________________

Pets

1. ______________________________

2. ______________________________

3. ______________________________

Strangers

1. ______________________________

2. ______________________________

3. ______________________________

Nature

1. ______________________________

2. ______________________________

3. ______________________________

Day 16

31 Day Hug Journal

☺ Folks, your goal is *twelve* :20-daily-hugs at minimum

☺ Seven Huggee Groups;
Self | Kids | Partner | Friends | Pets | Strangers | Nature

☺ Pick three daily times | Jot down who got the hug by name | Jot down how you/recipient felt after the hug

Self

1. ______________________________

2. ______________________________

3. ______________________________

Kids

1. ______________________________

2. ______________________________

3. ______________________________

Partner

1. ______________________________

2. ______________________________

3. ______________________________

Friends

1. ______________________________

2. ______________________________

3. ______________________________

Pets

1. ______________________________

2. ______________________________

3. ______________________________

Strangers

1. ______________________________

2. ______________________________

3. ______________________________

Nature

1. ______________________________

2. ______________________________

3. ______________________________

Day 17

31 Day Hug Journal

☺ Folks, your goal is *twelve* :20-daily-hugs at minimum

☺ Seven Huggee Groups;
Self | Kids | Partner | Friends | Pets | Strangers | Nature

☺ Pick three daily times | Jot down who got the hug by name | Jot down how you/recipient felt after the hug

Self

1. ____________________________________

2. ____________________________________

3. ____________________________________

Kids

1. ____________________________________

2. ____________________________________

3. ____________________________________

Partner

1. ____________________________________

2. ____________________________________

3. ____________________________________

Friends

1. ______________________________

2. ______________________________

3. ______________________________

Pets

1. ______________________________

2. ______________________________

3. ______________________________

Strangers

1. ______________________________

2. ______________________________

3. ______________________________

Nature

1. ______________________________

2. ______________________________

3. ______________________________

Day 18

31 Day Hug Journal

☺ Folks, your goal is *twelve* :20-daily-hugs at minimum

☺ Seven Huggee Groups;
Self | Kids | Partner | Friends | Pets | Strangers | Nature

☺ Pick three daily times | Jot down who got the hug by name | Jot down how you/recipient felt after the hug

Self

1. ______________________________

2. ______________________________

3. ______________________________

Kids

1. ______________________________

2. ______________________________

3. ______________________________

Partner

1. ______________________________

2. ______________________________

3. ______________________________

Friends

1. ____________________________________
2. ____________________________________
3. ____________________________________

Pets

1. ____________________________________
2. ____________________________________
3. ____________________________________

Strangers

1. ____________________________________
2. ____________________________________
3. ____________________________________

Nature

1. ____

2. ____

3. ____

Day 19

31 Day Hug Journal

☺ Folks, your goal is *twelve* :20-daily-hugs at minimum

☺ Seven Huggee Groups;
Self | Kids | Partner | Friends | Pets | Strangers | Nature

☺ Pick three daily times | Jot down who got the hug by name | Jot down how you/recipient felt after the hug

Self

1. ____

2. ____

3. ____

Kids

1. ____

2. ____

3. ____

Partner

1. ____

2. ____

3. ____

Friends

1. ____________________________________
2. ____________________________________
3. ____________________________________

Pets

1. ____________________________________
2. ____________________________________
3. ____________________________________

Strangers

1. ____________________________________
2. ____________________________________
3. ____________________________________

Nature

1. ______________________________

2. ______________________________

3. ______________________________

Day 20

31 Day Hug Journal

☺ Folks, your goal is *twelve* :20-daily-hugs at minimum

☺ Seven Huggee Groups;
Self | Kids | Partner | Friends | Pets | Strangers | Nature

☺ Pick three daily times | Jot down who got the hug by name | Jot down how you/recipient felt after the hug

Self

1. ______________________________

2. ______________________________

3. ______________________________

Kids

1. ______________________________

2. ______________________________

3. ______________________________

Partner

1. ______________________________

2. ______________________________

3. ______________________________

Friends

1. ______________________________

2. ______________________________

3. ______________________________

Pets

1. ______________________________

2. ______________________________

3. ______________________________

Strangers

1. ______________________________

2. ______________________________

3. ______________________________

Nature

1. ______________________________

2. ______________________________

3. ______________________________

Day 21

31 Day Hug Journal

☺ Folks, your goal is *twelve* :20-daily-hugs at minimum

☺ Seven Huggee Groups;
Self | Kids | Partner | Friends | Pets | Strangers | Nature

☺ Pick three daily times | Jot down who got the hug by name | Jot down how you/recipient felt after the hug

Self

1. ______________________________

2. ______________________________

3. ______________________________

Kids

1. ______________________________

2. ______________________________

3. ______________________________

Partner

1. ______________________________

2. ______________________________

3. ______________________________

Friends

1. ____________________

2. ____________________

3. ____________________

Pets

1. ____________________

2. ____________________

3. ____________________

Strangers

1. ____________________

2. ____________________

3. ____________________

Nature

1. ______________________________

2. ______________________________

3. ______________________________

Day 22

31 Day Hug Journal

☺ Folks, your goal is *twelve* :20-daily-hugs at minimum

☺ Seven Huggee Groups;
Self | Kids | Partner | Friends | Pets | Strangers | Nature

☺ Pick three daily times | Jot down who got the hug by name | Jot down how you/recipient felt after the hug

Self

1. ____
2. ____
3. ____

Kids

1. ____
2. ____
3. ____

Partner

1. ____
2. ____
3. ____

Friends

1. ____________________

2. ____________________

3. ____________________

Pets

1. ____________________

2. ____________________

3. ____________________

Strangers

1. ____________________

2. ____________________

3. ____________________

Nature

1. ______________________________

2. ______________________________

3. ______________________________

Day 23

31 Day Hug Journal

☺ Folks, your goal is *twelve* :20-daily-hugs at minimum

☺ Seven Huggee Groups;
Self | Kids | Partner | Friends | Pets | Strangers | Nature

☺ Pick three daily times | Jot down who got the hug by name | Jot down how you/recipient felt after the hug

Self

1. ______________________________

2. ______________________________

3. ______________________________

Kids

1. ______________________________

2. ______________________________

3. ______________________________

Partner

1. ______________________________

2. ______________________________

3. ______________________________

Friends

1. ____

2. ____

3. ____

Pets

1. ____

2. ____

3. ____

Strangers

1. ____

2. ____

3. ____

Nature

1. ______________________________

2. ______________________________

3. ______________________________

Day 24

31 Day Hug Journal

☺ Folks, your goal is *twelve* :20-daily-hugs at minimum

☺ Seven Huggee Groups;
Self | Kids | Partner | Friends | Pets | Strangers | Nature

☺ Pick three daily times | Jot down who got the hug by name | Jot down how you/recipient felt after the hug

Self

1. ______________________________

2. ______________________________

3. ______________________________

Kids

1. ______________________________

2. ______________________________

3. ______________________________

Partner

1. ______________________________

2. ______________________________

3. ______________________________

Friends

1. ______________________________

2. ______________________________

3. ______________________________

Pets

1. ______________________________

2. ______________________________

3. ______________________________

Strangers

1. ______________________________

2. ______________________________

3. ______________________________

Nature

1. ______________________________

2. ______________________________

3. ______________________________

Day 25

31 Day Hug Journal

☺ Folks, your goal is *twelve* :20-daily-hugs at minimum

☺ Seven Huggee Groups;
Self | Kids | Partner | Friends | Pets | Strangers | Nature

☺ Pick three daily times | Jot down who got the hug by name | Jot down how you/recipient felt after the hug

Self

1. ____________________

2. ____________________

3. ____________________

Kids

1. ____________________

2. ____________________

3. ____________________

Partner

1. ____________________

2. ____________________

3. ____________________

Friends

1. ______________________________

2. ______________________________

3. ______________________________

Pets

1. ______________________________

2. ______________________________

3. ______________________________

Strangers

1. ______________________________

2. ______________________________

3. ______________________________

Nature

1. ______________________________

2. ______________________________

3. ______________________________

Day 26

31 Day Hug Journal

☺ Folks, your goal is *twelve* :20-daily-hugs at minimum

☺ Seven Huggee Groups;
Self | Kids | Partner | Friends | Pets | Strangers | Nature

☺ Pick three daily times | Jot down who got the hug by name | Jot down how you/recipient felt after the hug

Self

1. ______________________________

2. ______________________________

3. ______________________________

Kids

1. ______________________________

2. ______________________________

3. ______________________________

Partner

1. ______________________________

2. ______________________________

3. ______________________________

Friends

1. ______________________________

2. ______________________________

3. ______________________________

Pets

1. ______________________________

2. ______________________________

3. ______________________________

Strangers

1. ______________________________

2. ______________________________

3. ______________________________

Nature

1. ______________________________

2. ______________________________

3. ______________________________

Day 27

31 Day Hug Journal

☺ Folks, your goal is *twelve* :20-daily-hugs at minimum

☺ Seven Huggee Groups;
Self | Kids | Partner | Friends | Pets | Strangers | Nature

☺ Pick three daily times | Jot down who got the hug by name | Jot down how you/recipient felt after the hug

Self

1. ______________________________

2. ______________________________

3. ______________________________

Kids

1. ______________________________

2. ______________________________

3. ______________________________

Partner

1. ______________________________

2. ______________________________

3. ______________________________

Friends

1. ______________________________

2. ______________________________

3. ______________________________

Pets

1. ______________________________

2. ______________________________

3. ______________________________

Strangers

1. ______________________________

2. ______________________________

3. ______________________________

Nature

1. ______________________________

2. ______________________________

3. ______________________________

Day 28

31 Day Hug Journal

☺ Folks, your goal is *twelve* :20-daily-hugs at minimum

☺ Seven Huggee Groups;
Self | Kids | Partner | Friends | Pets | Strangers | Nature

☺ Pick three daily times | Jot down who got the hug by name | Jot down how you/recipient felt after the hug

Self

1. ______________________________

2. ______________________________

3. ______________________________

Kids

1. ______________________________

2. ______________________________

3. ______________________________

Partner

1. ______________________________

2. ______________________________

3. ______________________________

Friends

1. ______________________________

2. ______________________________

3. ______________________________

Pets

1. ______________________________

2. ______________________________

3. ______________________________

Strangers

1. ______________________________

2. ______________________________

3. ______________________________

Nature

1. ______________________________

2. ______________________________

3. ______________________________

Day 29

31 Day Hug Journal

☺ Folks, your goal is *twelve* :20-daily-hugs at minimum

☺ Seven Huggee Groups;
Self | Kids | Partner | Friends | Pets | Strangers | Nature

☺ Pick three daily times | Jot down who got the hug by name | Jot down how you/recipient felt after the hug

Self

1. ______________________________

2. ______________________________

3. ______________________________

Kids

1. ______________________________

2. ______________________________

3. ______________________________

Partner

1. ______________________________

2. ______________________________

3. ______________________________

Friends

1. ______________________________

2. ______________________________

3. ______________________________

Pets

1. ______________________________

2. ______________________________

3. ______________________________

Strangers

1. ______________________________

2. ______________________________

3. ______________________________

Nature

1. ____________________

2. ____________________

3. ____________________

Day 30

31 Day Hug Journal

☺ Folks, your goal is *twelve* :20-daily-hugs at minimum

☺ Seven Huggee Groups;
Self | Kids | Partner | Friends | Pets | Strangers | Nature

☺ Pick three daily times | Jot down who got the hug by name | Jot down how you/recipient felt after the hug

Self

1. ________________________________
2. ________________________________
3. ________________________________

Kids

1. ________________________________
2. ________________________________
3. ________________________________

Partner

1. ________________________________
2. ________________________________
3. ________________________________

Friends

1. ____

2. ____

3. ____

Pets

1. ____

2. ____

3. ____

Strangers

1. ____

2. ____

3. ____

Nature

1. ______________________________

2. ______________________________

3. ______________________________

Day 31

31 Day Hug Journal

☺ Folks, your goal is *twelve* :20-daily-hugs at minimum

☺ Seven Huggee Groups;
Self | Kids | Partner | Friends | Pets | Strangers | Nature

☺ Pick three daily times | Jot down who got the hug by name | Jot down how you/recipient felt after the hug

Self

1. ______________________________

2. ______________________________

3. ______________________________

Kids

1. ______________________________

2. ______________________________

3. ______________________________

Partner

1. ______________________________

2. ______________________________

3. ______________________________

Friends

1. ______________________________

2. ______________________________

3. ______________________________

Pets

1. ______________________________

2. ______________________________

3. ______________________________

Strangers

1. ______________________________

2. ______________________________

3. ______________________________

Nature

1. ______________________________

2. ______________________________

3. ______________________________

www.ingramcontent.com/pod-product-compliance
Lightning Source LLC
Chambersburg PA
CBHW051941090426
42741CB00008B/1222
* 9 7 8 0 6 9 2 7 8 0 8 3 1 *